David Williamson was born
up in Bairnsdale, north-eastern Victoria. He is a graduate in
Mechanical Engineering from Monash University and was a
lecturer in thermo-dynamics and social psychology at
Swinburn Institute of Technology until 1973. His first
full-length play, *The Coming of Stork*, had its premiere at the
La Mama Theatre, Carlton, in 1970 and later became the film
Stork, directed by Tim Burstall.

But it was his next two plays which together established
him as Australia's most sought-after dramatic writer. *The
Removalists* and *Don's Party*, both written in 1971, were
quickly taken up and performed around Australia, then in
London and later made into films with screenplays by the
author. *The Removalists* won the British George Devine Award
in 1971 for the Nimrod Street production in Sydney; and in
1972 the Australian Writers Guild Awgie Awards for the best
stage play and the best script in any medium. In 1973 David
Williamson was nominated the most promising playwright by
the London *Evening Standard* following the British production
of *The Removalists*.

The next play was *Jugglers Three* (1972) commissioned by
the Melbourne Theatre Company; followed by *What If You
Died Tomorrow* (1973) for the Old Tote Theatre Company;
The Department (1975) and *A Handful of Friends* (1976) for
the South Australian Theatre Company. *The Club* (1977) broke
all previous box office records and in 1978 had seasons at
the Kennedy Centre, Washington, on Broadway and in Berlin.
In 1980 the Nimrod Theatre production went to London. The
film, directed by Bruce Beresford, was released in 1980.
Travelling North was performed around Australia in 1979 and
in London in 1980. The film version was released in 1987.
It was followed by *Celluloid Heroes* (1980), *The Perfectionist*
(1982), *Sons of Cain* (1985) and *Emerald City* (1987). The
film version of *Emerald City* was released in 1989. *Top Silk*
was first produced in Sydney and Melbourne in 1989. *Siren*
was produced in Sydney and Melbourne in 1990.

David Williamson has won the Australian Film Institute
film script award for *Petersen* (1974), *Don's Party* (1976),
Gallipoli (1981) and *Travelling North* (1987). He lives in
Sydney with his journalist wife Kristin and four children.

Also by David Williamson:

The Removalists
Don's Party
The Department
A Handful of Friends
The Club
Travelling North
The Perfectionist
Sons of Cain
Collected Plays Volume 1:
　　The Coming of Stork
　　Don's Party
　　The Removalists
　　Jugglers Three
　　What if you Died Tomorrow
Emerald City
Top Silk

SIREN

David Williamson

CURRENCY PRESS • SYDNEY

CURRENCY PLAYS
General Editor: Katharine Brisbane

First published in 1991 by
Currency Press Ltd
P.O. Box 452, Paddington NSW 2021 Australia

National Library of Australia
Cataloguing-in-Publication data
Williamson, David, 1942-
  Siren

  ISBN 0 86819 282 1
  I. Title.
A822.3

Typeset by Allette Systems Pty Ltd, Sydney.
Printed by Southwood Press, Marrickville, N.S.W.
Cover photo shows Andrea Moore, photo by Gary Heery
Cover design by Trevor Hood.

Andrea Moor as Liz and John Walton as Paul in the Sydney Theatre Company production of *Siren*, 1990. Photographer: Stuart Campbell.

Above: Tony Poli as Kostas and Rob Steele as Billy in the Sydney Theatre Company production of *Siren*, 1990. Photographer: Stuart Campbell. Below: Tony Poli as Kostas and William Zappa as Rob in the same production. Photographer: Stuart Campbell.

Contents

Above: Mike Bishop as Rob and Jean Kittson as Liz in the Elston, Hocking and Woods production of *Siren*, 1990. Photographer: Jeff Busby. Below: Nick Carrafa as Kostas and Tracy Harvey as Sharon in the same production. Photographer: Jeff Busby.

A Return To The Elements

Katharine Brisbane

Siren represents a new departure for David Williamson, or rather a development of his work in a direction which, though latent in his more recent plays, nevertheless had the power to surprise and confuse his critics. And in another way it is a return to the elements of confrontation drama and role-playing which characterised his early work.

Siren is a frank situation comedy employing the devices of farce and the old morality plays. Here we have the Vices holed up in a Central Coast motel preying upon each other and the townspeople. Those who look for the development of character which informs Travelling North will not find it here, nor the passionate concern with corruption or political belief that we find in Don's Party and Sons of Cain (though corruption is the catalyst in Siren). Nor do we find the emotive imagery on which Jugglers Three or What If You Died Tomorrow are constructed. This time Williamson has chosen to take another look, and in a quite different style, at the games of powerplay which he addressed in The Removalists and later in The Department, The Club and The Perfectionist. The style is nearer to Emerald City than any of his earlier plays. And the game is sexual politics.

Liz is the siren holed up with three undercover detectives. She has been employed to use her sex appeal upon Billy Nottle, a local councillor suspected of taking bribes from developers. At the time of writing the question of corruption behind the bulldozing of pristine stretches of Australia's coastal and wilderness regions was in public debate; but it is not Avarice who claims Williamson's attention. It is the equally despoiling Covetousness, a 'conquest junkie' who cannot help herself. Liz is a compulsive sexual predator who sees herself as a victim of love; and she is hoping the covert operation will cure her feelings of inadequacy by proving she is 'good at something.' In fact she has been employed for her sex appeal.

But there is another aspect of Liz's personality which takes us back to *The Removalists*. Liz is 'classy', 'the product of three generations of ear, nose and throat specialists and you can't get classier than that'. It's as if the character of Kate Mason, the dentist's wife ('same money, less prestige' says Sergeant Simmonds, comparing her husband's profession with that of medicine) has haunted Williamson for twenty years and demanded further examination. Kate presented for Simmonds the same sexual challenge with which Kostas, the working-class Greek, is confronted in *Siren*. Williamson's examination does not, however, take him into the psychology of Kate and Liz's promiscuity but, as in any good morality play, into its mechanics and its consequences.

The failure of a hidden tape recorder at Liz's first interview with Nottle is the device on which the action of the play swings. Three heterosexual men (one might call them Wrath, Envy and Lechery) are left with time on their hands awaiting the setting of a second trap. There follows a skilfully orchestrated series of seduction scenes, involving all four and the receptionist, in which the motivations are eroticism and self-deception. The purpose in writing the play, Williamson has said, was to show how ridiculous human beings could become when we tried to juggle sex, power and ego.

Faced with this highly erotic material, he balances it with a cerebral form. Since *The Perfectionist* he has made fairly regular use of direct address to the audience but here he integrates the device for the first time into the action, tempting the audience to join the emotional game before setting them back sharply on their wits with a smart aside. There is no subtext to this work. The characters are archetypes of deviousness and they share their deviousness with us transparently. There is also no social context in the way we have come to expect from Williamson, but there is a moral one. The motel too is an archetype: it belongs to the age-old world of theatrical convention. But being like every other motel in the world, and every motel bedroom resembling the next, it becomes a symbol of the debasement of values. 'Whatever happened to love!' asks the gullible Sharon. 'Love is something they sing about in pop songs', replies Liz flippantly.

There are three levels of reality on which the actors play: the characters' roles to outsiders, from whom they are hiding their real identity; their competitive role-playing among themselves; and brief glimpses of their private selves.

The play opens with Liz addressing the audience. As a child, she disarmingly tells us, she took pleasure from wickedness and twisting her father round her little finger: '...the thought entered my mind: 'Maybe all men are idiots.' I guess that's a thought that's never quite left me.'

She is followed by Paul, the senior detective, looking back on the events which are about to unfold: 'I had a nagging feeling the whole operation was going to be a stuff up, but I had no idea of the dimensions.' And then Kostas, opening the first round with Billy Nottle: '[to audience] I'd been getting nowhere with Billy...'

What follows is in the same broad style: explication and motivation are spelt out as Liz, assuming the role of a developer's wife, works the scene up to a fever pitch forcing the wily Nottle to drop his notebook, to which he has prudently been confining his replies, and provide some verbal evidence of their transaction on tape.

LIZ: You know something? I'd rather ditch the whole project that pay money to a sleazebag like you!
BILLY: You can forget your permit, lady. You've just blown the deal. [Exit.]

It's the language of melodrama and sit-com; an engineered argument, a powerplay. The scene is followed by a more realistic one as the team come to terms with the fact that their hidden tape-recorder has failed to record.

All this may appear simple, even artless, and yet what Williamson is demanding of his actors is extremely sophisticated: the precision of artifice. On the page the shading of difference between the role-playing argument and the real one is not so striking. In performance it is vastly significant because on it hangs the whole balance of the play.

The chief clue to the role-playing is the direct address to the audience. The play begins with two characters explaining themselves (previous drafts had all the characters lined up to confide their moral qualities); and both acts end in similar fashion. Within each scene are further asides, each coming at a moment of high feeling, cutting across it and reminding us in the audience that these familiar human emotions are yet another example of role-playing, conscious or unconscious; that for skilled manipulators like this team accepted human values are a commodity. It is a Brechtian device to repeatedly distance the audience from the emotions being conjured up and to require their judgement upon a scene only too familiar to us from popular fiction. It is also a comic device with a much older history.

Sharon, the 'check-in chick', is a gull straight out of that history. She has been seduced away from her dull fiancé by Kostas, and is taken in by his pretence of love. She is the most purely farcical character in the play, taking as she does to farcical solutions to her desperation. We are sorry for Sharon, who marries her Greg, but her romantic view of love, in Williamson's view, has no more staying power than Liz's passing conquests.

Despite the growth of our theatre in the last twenty years, the skills required for this kind of play remain rare among our actors. They are those of the personality performer, not the realist actor; the comedy star whom one admires not for their insights into character but for their craftsmanship. Modern Australian comedy has tended to take the bushfire rather than the laser beam to its target. It's a rough and ready form of assaulting the audience. Williamson's writing is elegant and economical and it demands a much more subtle execution.

Siren opened with two simultaneous premieres in Melbourne and Sydney on 22 March 1990 and the widely varying press accounts of both productions following the high-powered marketing campaigns give an insight into the dilemma which expectations of a new Williamson play can cause. The Melbourne reviewers for the most part were looking for naturalistic social commentary and finding it obscure. Some found the characters unsympathetic and dismissed the concept of farce pejoratively. They appeared confused by the style, by the mixture of apparent naturalism and direct address to the audience; and Alison Croggon in the *Bulletin* (3 April) saw an attempt at a feminist critique which only reinforced old behaviour patterns. 'Women don't believe any more that the only power they have is sexual power over men.' She also found Williamson 'doubtful of the society in which he lives and uncertain of how to write about it.'

Helen Thomson in the *Sunday Herald* (25 March) took a more persuasive approach:

David Williamson's latest play is a new chapter in his continuing love affair with audiences and troubled stand-off with professional critics. Siren shows people how they are, but not how they ought to be.

The play invites audiences to judge its deeply flawed characters but stands back from judgement itself. It's all about sex, but it knows that power is the most irresistible aphrodisiac of all.

Siren is certainly clever in its way. Williamson's dialogue is as sharp and funny as ever. The play is neatly put together; its second half a tangled bedroom farce that might have done credit to a Restoration dramatist. The characters could serve as a fairly complete sample of the ancient Vices.

In Sydney the reviewers' search for psychological depth and truth also proved unfruitful and the production revealed a mixture of styles. Frank Gauntlett in the *Daily Mirror* (27 March) summed up the impact of the play on the audience: 'the audience is addressed directly and often with alarming candor, rude farce jostles with situation comedy, sharp social comment sucks against rough caricature; we are frequently buffeted by uncertain eddies of humor - should we laugh at, with or at all?' Brian Hoad in the *Bulletin* (3 April) defined the tension within the production of farcical form and serious comic intent and concluded that 'with funnier scenery, fewer clothes and more explicit choreography *Siren* could easily become the soft porn sensation of the season.'

It is clear from the reviews that these early productions did not exploit the levels of role-playing within the play or manage to make a coherent style in performance. Nor could the majority of reviewers successfully distinguish between text and performance or define the author's intent and achievement convincingly.

Siren is, according to Liz in the last line of the play, 'a contemporary love story of sorts'. And so it is, though the message is a harsh one and proved unacceptable to critics of the early productions. The play is, finally, an indictment of contemporary Australia as the creator of insulated pockets of corruption like this one in which greed is allowed to reduce human motivation to the ridiculous. Sex is Williamson's metaphor but Covetousness is the theme. To bring a corrupt councillor to justice may be the avowed purpose of the group but when he is nailed they turn upon each other, taking revenge for personal betrayals in the name of the law.

It is only in the final rapprochement between Liz and Kostas that their private selves begin to emerge and the direct address stops interrupting them. In the comedy convention Liz chooses the unexpected partner, the one who shares her own weaknesses. And in a final echo of *The Removalists* - Simmonds' fond working-class belief that the rich exercise certain social responsibilities - Kostas too has to come to terms with his hang-up about class; about aristocratic women and exploiters who are 'poison'. From this point in the play they both begin to act with a new sense of reality. Love, they tentatively begin to discover, is not exploitation but demands honesty, consideration, trust and self-control. It's a beginning, says Williamson, the eternal optimist. Even in this rotten world human values will insist on revealing themselves, showing up the siren songs of the commodity culture as sterile illusions.

Their masks off, the characters finish their story, embrace the audience and unmask the whole work, in the same way the play began, as the harmless fabrication of a bunch of players. for after all *Siren* is a situation comedy, and a love story - of sorts.

Andrea Moor as Liz and William Zappa as Rob in the Sydney Theatre Company production of *Siren*, 1990. Photographer: Stuart Campbell.

Above: Nick Carrafa as Kostas and Roy Baldwin as Billy in the Elston, Hocking and Woods production of *Siren*, 1990. Photographer: Jeff Busby. Below: Jeanette Cronin as Sharon in the Sydney Theatre Company production of *Siren*, 1990. Photographer: Stuart Campbell.

Siren was first produced in both Sydney and Melbourne on 22nd March, 1990 by the Sydney Theatre Company and by Elston, Hocking and Woods and Kinselas Productions respectively with the following casts:

Sydney production at the Wharf

LIZ	Andrea Moor
PAUL	John Walton
KOSTAS	Tony Poli
BILLY NOTTLE	Rob Steele
ROB	William Zappa
SHARON	Jeanette Cronin
STEVEN	D.J. Foster

Directed by Richard Wherrett
Dramaturg: May-Brit Akerholt
Set Designer: D4 Design
Costume Designer: Sarah Tooth
Lighting Designer: Neil Finlayson
Stage Manager: Jenny Ward
Production Photographer: Stuart Campbell

Melbourne production at the Athenaeum Theatre

LIZ	Jean Kittson
PAUL	John Orcsik
KOSTAS	Nick Carrafa
BILLY NOTTLE	Roy Baldwin
ROB	Mike Bishop
SHARON	Tracy Harvey
STEVEN	Peter Flett

Directed by Graeme Blundell
Designed by Richard Roberts
Production Photographer: Jeff Busby

CHARACTERS

LIZ
PAUL
KOSTAS
BILLY NOTTLE
PAUL
ROB
SHARON
STEVEN

SETTING

The action takes place in a motel.

ACT ONE

Blackout. Lights up. LIZ *walks onstage and looks at the audience. She's in her mid to late twenties, is very attractive and warmly personable.*

LIZ: [*to audience*] When I was five or six I liked being bad so much that I began to think I'd been sent to earth by the devil. I could twist my father round my little finger. All I had to do was bat my eyes, smile and I got whatever I wanted. I remember thinking 'Dad's an idiot', and wondering when he was going to put his foot down and stop me. He never did, so the thought entered my mind, 'Maybe all men are idiots', and I guess that's a thought that's never quite left me.

> [PAUL, *a tough handsome man in his late thirties steps forward. He watches* LIZ *as she passes and moves offstage, then points to* BILLY NOTTLE, *a ferret of a man in his fifties, who sits in a chair.*]

PAUL: I had a nagging feeling the whole operation was going to be a stuff up, but I had no idea of the dimensions. The irony is Billy Nottle was small beer. A local mayor pushing dubious developments through council for a few thousand dollars a time. I wanted to get him. He'd let developers build tacky motels on some of the most beautiful sites on the southern coast, but catching him wasn't going to be easy. He had a rat like cunning. He knew some one would eventually come after him with tape recorders hidden in their lapels so he never spoke business out loud. He wrote everything on a pad and tore it up immediately. And we'd never catch him accepting money. He'd set an elaborate delivery chain and all we'd ever get if we moved was one of the links. The only way was to get him to talk. Out loud.

> [*Lights fade and come up on a motel room. It's not exactly seedy, but its decor jars. A tacky commercial painting adorns the wall, and the colours, carpets and fittings are provincial Australia with faint Spanish overtones. A ferret like man in his fifties,* BILLY NOTTLE,

sits in a chair. KOSTAS *walks around him, trying to sell him a course of action. It's early afternoon.*]

KOSTAS: [*to audience*] I'd been getting nowhere with Billy. He was more than willing to do the deal, but nothing I could do could get him to talk. And I was running out of reasons not to pay him the money. So we'd invented my 'wife'. My background had been fabricated, but everything checked out. We did the same with Liz. That side of it was all very professional.

Billy, I'd leave the money where ever you said. Right now. I'm convinced you have the council in the palm of your hand, but Sheena isn't. All she needs is a bit of reassurance that we won't be blowing the down payment.

[BILLY *hesitates.*]

See her, tell me where and how you want the money left, and you'll have the first payment within hours.

[BILLY *nods.*]

[KOSTAS *relieved, moves to the door*] All she wants is reassurance, O.K?

[*He opens the door, looks down the corridor and beckons someone.* LIZ *enters.*]

Billy, this is my wife Sheena. I'll leave you two to talk.

[*He goes out closing the door.*]

LIZ: Mr Nottle. Before we give you fifty thousand dollars I just want to know how you're going to convince your other nine council members to let our application through when it's clearly in breach of council zoning laws.

[BILLY *begins to write something on paper.* LIZ *gets angry.*]

Mr Nottle, this is ridiculous. You've checked out our bona fides, you know we're genuine. For heavens sake put down that pencil and speak to me!

[BILLY *screws up that sheet and writes something else. He shows it to her. She reads.*]

'If you don't want to do business with me you don't have to.' [*Pause. She glares.*] Mr Nottle, I would love not to have to do business with you, but it seems we have no choice. How can you guarantee you'll get council to approve our application?

[BILLY *writes something and shows it to her.*]
You have the numbers. [*Nods*] You spread the money round
a bit?
[BILLY *writes something.* LIZ *reads it.*]
More or less? So half the council is on the take? That's
what you're saying?
[BILLY *writes something.* LIZ *reads it.*]
You can't stop progress. You're realists? Ah, that's what
it's called these days. Realism. Well Mr Nottle, we'll pay
the first twenty thousand. And the rest when it happens,
but I just want you to know one thing. As far as I'm
concerned you're a sleazebag, and if there was any way I
could put a curse to ensure that your life was as happy as
a cane toad in a plastic bag in a deep freeze, I would do
it.
[BILLY *begins writing angrily on his pad.* LIZ *picks up
the pad and hurls it into the corner.*]
What are you? A man or a worm! If you're going to try
and defend yourself, have the guts to speak! Have the guts
to speak!
BILLY: [*angrily*] Listen lady, you came to me, I didn't come
to you. You want to build a ten storey development in a
rural zoning, then pay up or forget it.
LIZ: This area needs developments like this. If your whole
rotten council wasn't corrupt we wouldn't have to pay a
fifty thousand dollar bribe, we'd be welcomed!
BILLY: Lady, I'm too old to listen to lectures on morals. You
want something, you pay. End of discussion.
LIZ: Don't you have any conscience about using a position of
public trust for private gain?
BILLY: Listen lady, I wasn't born on easy street. I didn't have
a Dad who left me millions like you two. Billy Nottle has
had to fight for every bloody cent he's ever made, because
if your old man's just a battler like mine was, then you're
out on your own and if you don't look after yourself no
other bastard is going to.
LIZ: There are a lot of other kids from poor backgrounds
who've made it without resorting to graft.
BILLY: Bully for them. Now pay up or piss off.

LIZ: You know something? I'd rather ditch the whole project than pay money to a sleazebag like you!

BILLY: You can forget your permit lady. You've just blown the deal.

[*He walks out and slams the door after him. The lights fade and go up again. We're now in* PAUL's *room which is identical to* KOSTAS's *room except that the print on the wall is different. No more tasteful, but different.* PAUL *is pacing around the room, furious. It's early afternoon. The object of his fury,* ROB *is looking sullen.* KOSTAS *and* LIZ *are also furious, but they are leaving it to* PAUL *to do the shouting. A tape recorder sits on the bed.*]

PAUL: It stems pretty fundamental to me that if you take hours to wire someone up, you check the batteries!

ROB: The batteries were brand new. The operating light was on, the spools turned, the voice check worked.

PAUL: How come Liz starts speaking an octave higher than normal and by the time Nottle finally opens his mouth we hear one faint squeak!

KOSTAS: Batteries have a shelf life just like anything else. They'd been probably sitting there for years.

ROB: How the fuck was I supposed to know that!

PAUL: You test them!

ROB: With what?

KOSTAS: With a meter. It's there in the equipment.

LIZ: I can't believe this. I got him to say everything. Even his name.

PAUL: The fact he was taking a bribe?

LIZ: [*nods*] And the fact that half the council is on the take as well.

PAUL: [*groans*] Jesus!

ROB: [*to* PAUL] You could've checked the batteries.

PAUL: [*to* ROB] I can't leave one thing to you?

ROB: I'm sorry. Mea Culpa. What do you want me to do? Put a gun to my head?

KOSTAS: Why bother. You've been brain dead for years.

[ROB *is not amused. He moves towards* KOSTAS *menacingly.* PAUL *intervenes.*]

PAUL: We're not going to get anywhere yelling at each other. We'll just have to try it again.

LIZ: I got him to talk once. I can do it again.

KOSTAS: Liz, I was outside the door. You yelled at him and he walked out. There's no way he's going to talk to you again.

LIZ: I didn't call him anything really insulting.

KOSTAS: Liz, I know there's a cultural lag down here, but they do know that sleazebag doesn't mean honeybaby!

LIZ: Tell him you've given me a thrashing and I'm ready to grovel.

KOSTAS: I look the sort of guy who thrashes his wife?

LIZ: You're Greek.

KOSTAS: We're doing ethnic insults now are we? Why can't you give an Australian a lunch break longer than twenty minutes? Because if you do he has to be sent for job retraining. I got a thousand more.

PAUL: Kostas - -

KOSTAS: [to PAUL] How am I expected to get Billy Nottle back in here when she shrieks at him!

LIZ: Tell him it was P.M.T. Normally I'm a sweetie. Tell him anything. Just get him back in the room and I'll do the rest.

KOSTAS: [angry] You do everything wrong last time and get lucky and suddenly you're the expert!

LIZ: [angry] I knew exactly what I was doing last time and I can do it again.

KOSTAS: If the recorder had've been loaded with live batteries we wouldn't have to do it again!

LIZ: [to KOSTAS] It's not going to get us anywhere to keep blaming Rob! You take batteries off the shelf, you assume they're going to work.

ROB: Thank you.

KOSTAS: [angry] We're not going to get Nottle in here again!

PAUL: You're going to have to try. We've got no other option.
    [ROB steps forward.]

ROB: [He stares at PAUL and KOSTAS] Batman and Robin. The masked avengers. Paul and I started out together in police training school. I came first, he came second, but from that

moment on it has always been the other way. He was the youngest Inspector ever appointed. Before him you had to be fifty five and be able to organise criminal activity on a shared profit basis. Not that 'Mr Clean' - [*he indicates* PAUL] was entirely clean, but we'll get to that later. When we were still both cops, I was better at it than he was. I was the best interrogator in the force. I could make flint hard psychopaths weep out confessions. I was brilliant. But Paul got the promotions. So where's the justice in life? The simple answer is that there isn't any. I started my law course a year before he did, I got honours all the way, he scraped through. We both apply to head up the Task Force against Corruption, T.F.A.C., and who gets it - Him. I get the number two job on appeal. As for Kostas - [*he looks at* KOSTAS]
Look at his clothes. Who but a dead set ponce would dress like that?

[*He looks at* KOSTAS *again*]
And he's got an arts-law degree and women fall over themselves to get into bed with him, and he's doing an M.B.A., and he makes jokes that are funnier than mine.

[*The lights fade. They go up again.* PAUL *is sitting, dejected in his room.* KOSTAS *is patrolling around restlessly. Late afternoon.*]

PAUL: Can you believe it? We finally get the little weasel to talk, and - -

KOSTAS: We'll get him.

PAUL: Who cares?

KOSTAS: I care. He's a little turd. Have you seen the plans of this development Liz and I are supposed to be building? [PAUL *nods*] The architect who drew it up for us said he felt as if he had committed a crime against humanity just putting it on paper. For fifty thousand these guys would let it be built.

PAUL: I was stupid to take on this job.

KOSTAS: Hey come on. What is this? One mistake and you want to give up?

PAUL: This task force was set up as a political exercise. To win a few extra votes.

KOSTAS: There was an element of that.

PAUL: We're window dressing mate. Maximum publicity and minimum resources. And I was stupid enough to get sucked in.

KOSTAS: Mate, we're just about to catch a nasty little grafter and four or five of his mates.

PAUL: And that's as far as we're ever going to get.

KOSTAS: We started the insider trading investigation.

PAUL: Yeah, then had to hand it over to the fraud squad because we haven't got the manpower. The bastards got headlines for a week.

KOSTAS: [*nods*] And never once mentioned who - -

PAUL: And never once mentioned who put them onto it. Every time I turned on the television there was that moron Des Bartle taking all the credit. If I'd stayed in the force I'd've been heading up the fraud squad.

KOSTAS: Des is a disaster on the box. You can't take your eyes off that wart. You'd be distinct improvement.

PAUL: I couldn't give a shit about getting my head on television - -

KOSTAS: Hey, come on, when they didn't run that license racket piece on Sixty Minutes you sulked for a week.

PAUL: O.K. I like to be noticed. Most of us do.

KOSTAS: And you're stuck here in a backwater and it hurts?

PAUL: You can get out any time you like. You've got a thousand options.

KOSTAS: I don't want to get out. Not yet. I like catching the Billy Nottles of the world. It's like catching a cockroach. One of the world's great sounds -
   [*He mimes crushing a cockroach with his foot and makes the appropriate sound*]
   You know there are thousands more, but it's still great to get one. I did five years in a merchant bank and the most exciting thing I handled were my secretary's tits, and she enjoyed it more than I did.

PAUL: So why did you do it?

KOSTAS: She asked me to.

PAUL: You could've said no.

KOSTAS: She was a nice kid. I didn't want to hurt her feelings. And she could spell.

PAUL: You're having it off with the receptionist here, aren't you?

KOSTAS: No!

PAUL: I saw her coming out of your room. It's pretty bloody stupid indulging yourself when we're on an operation.

KOSTAS: There won't be any complications. I know how to handle women.

PAUL: When the hell are you going to settle down?

KOSTAS: Marriage, kids?

PAUL: [*sharply*] There's nothing wrong with marriage and kids.

KOSTAS: Did I say there was?

PAUL: The very best thing about my life is my family. You can sneer all you like - -

KOSTAS: I'm not sneering.

PAUL: Yes you are.

KOSTAS: Paul, I am going to get married. I am going to have children. I view it as a valid enterprise, but not yet.

PAUL: Why? Because you're having too much fun screwing everything that moves?

[KOSTAS *stares at him indignantly as if it's a monstrous suggestion*]

KOSTAS: Yes. Do I detect overtones of envy?

PAUL: Envy? That receptionist is an absolute dog. Dead set. Haven't you got any standards?

KOSTAS: Look out your window. It's a genetic disaster area.

PAUL: You've only been up here a week! Couldn't you stay away from women for a little while?

KOSTAS: Yes, but not a week.

PAUL: Do you ever think to yourself that screwing women you don't love is immature?

KOSTAS: I'd have to say it's a thought that hasn't often entered my head Paul, but I'll work on it.

PAUL: You've got a lot to learn.

KOSTAS: You're never tempted Paul?

PAUL: [*defensively*] I told you. I'm very happy with Helen and she's happy with me.

KOSTAS: So why'd hire Liz, eh?

PAUL: What d'you mean?

KOSTAS: Research Assistant? Even then she wasn't exactly qualified for the job. University drop out, never held down a job longer than a year —

PAUL: She had something about her. And I was right. She got Nottle to spill his guts.

KOSTAS: [*sharply*] And I didn't?

PAUL: I'm not saying that. It was probably luck.

KOSTAS: Mate, it was luck and nothing else but luck. You start abusing a guy like she did and nine times out of ten he's going to walk out without saying a word. And I mean it when I said I doubt if we're ever going to get him back again.

PAUL: O.K. It was luck. But she pulled it off. She's got something.

KOSTAS: Yeah, and you're not the only one that's ever noticed so just watch out.

PAUL: What do you mean?

KOSTAS: Mate, she's a killer. She's a fucking siren.

PAUL: Why do you hate her so much?

KOSTAS: I've seen 'em mate. I know how they operate. I read an article.

PAUL: About what?

KOSTAS: The siren syndrome. Women who lure married guys onto the rocks.

PAUL: Why?

KOSTAS: They hate men. Their uncle flashed at a family picnic, or their father left their doll out in the rain. Thousands of 'em. Sirens. She's one for sure.

PAUL: [*laughs*] You've just got it in for her.

KOSTAS: Mate, she's been giving you signals ever since she arrived and you are falling for it. You're being sucked in.

PAUL: Bullshit.

KOSTAS: [*doing a breathy imitation of* LIZ, *stroking his arm, staring into his eyes*] Paul, I know I haven't had the training but I really feel I could get him to talk.

PAUL: And she did, right? And you couldn't, right? And now you're pissed. O.K?

KOSTAS: All right. Don't listen. Go ahead and ruin your life.

PAUL: Mate, there is no way anything is ever going to happen between Liz and me. No way.

KOSTAS: [*to audience*] I really liked Paul. The code of communication between guys in this country doesn't exactly encourage intimacy, but I was sincerely trying to give him a warning.

PAUL: [*to audience*] I think I was in love with her even back then. I was trying to deny it to myself, but I was starting to feel things about her I'd never felt about anyone else. The depression as the weekends approached and I knew I wouldn't see her again till Monday. The ache in the chest and the almost uncontrollable impulse to move towards her when she walked into the room. Classic teenage symptoms. Only I'd never felt them then.

> [*Lights fade and go up again in* LIZ's *room. Evening.*]

LIZ: [*to audience*] I knew Paul was interested in me, and I guess I flirted. [*Pause*] I flirt with a lot of guys but they usually know the rules of the game. The problem was that stuff up with the batteries. If they hadn't been flat we would've had our evidence and been gone. They say your surroundings have a lot to do with your mood. It's not easy to sit around for days in identical tacky rooms without something happening. Even if only to relieve the boredom.

> [*The lights fade. They go up again. We're in* KOSTAS's *room. He's sitting there reading the Financial Review.* ROB *comes in. Late night. That same day.*]

ROB: Hi.

KOSTAS: Hi.

ROB: Is Nottle going to talk to you again?

KOSTAS: He's out of town for a few days. He said he'd ring when he gets back.

ROB: So we just sit here waiting.

> [KOSTAS *nods.*]

Sorry I stuffed up on the batteries.

KOSTAS: What am I supposed to say. That's O.K?

ROB: You never made a mistake?

KOSTAS: Not that sort of mistake.

ROB: Why don't you get yourself another room.

KOSTAS: Because I'm supposed to be sharing one with my 'wife'.

ROB: Yeah, well I'm not really enjoying you as a roommate.

KOSTAS: Likewise.

ROB: How did your front desk girl react when your 'wife' arrived?

KOSTAS: How do you think?

ROB: [*laughs*] No more room service?

[*There's a pause.* ROB *sits down and picks up the paper.* KOSTAS *continues to read.*]

We won't have to share after tonight.

KOSTAS: We can't book a new room. Sharon's on the front desk.

ROB: I'll be sharing a room with your 'wife'.

[KOSTAS *looks at him and roars laughing.*]

KOSTAS: Liz?

ROB: Pushover.

KOSTAS: Mate, hate to be the one to break the bad news, but if Liz has erotic dreams, you're not in them.

ROB: Let's have some money on that.

KOSTAS: Are you joking?

ROB: Say a hundred bucks. Liz and I will be an item before we leave. O.K?

KOSTAS: Sure. Go for it.

ROB: You think you're the only one who has any success with women? God's gift from Greece? Yeah, well think again.

KOSTAS: [*laughing*] Rob, face it. You've got more hope of getting laid by Mother Teresa.

[ROB *picks up the phone and dials.* KOSTAS *stares at him.*]

ROB: Liz? Rob. I've got to see you right now. In bed? At this hour? The night is a pup. Put on a dressing gown. I have to see you. It's very important.

[*There's a slight pause. He hangs up and turns to* KOSTAS *with a broad grin on his face.* KOSTAS *is frowning.*]

You may as well give me the hundred bucks right now. Got any condoms?

KOSTAS: They'd be no good for you. They're large size.

ROB: Where are they?

KOSTAS: Are you serious?

ROB: The ladies are choosy these days. If it's not on, it's not on.

[KOSTAS *fishes in the drawer and throws him a packet of condoms.*]

Only three?

[KOSTAS *shakes his head and laughs, but there's an edge of uneasiness in it.*]

[*to audience*] I wasn't quite as confident as I sounded, but I wanted to give that manicured arsehole a jolt. Anyone could have made it with that girl on the front desk. Poor kid. No one can help being born ugly, but the truth is a smile, a kind word - [*he shrugs*] anyone could have scored.

KOSTAS: [*to audience*] There's a certain type of woman I always assume is unavailable. Yeah, well if we're determined to be honest it's class based. Class is much more fluid in this country than most, but it's here. Liz comes from three generations of ear nose and throat specialists, and in this bloody country you can't do much better than that. My old man came out here from Greece to work in the Snowy mountains. My Mum is working class Oz. Liz had more money spent straightening her teeth than my old man earned. Liz? Unavailable. That's how I read her. Your father's a Greek Peasant. Hands off. That's how she projected. Then suddenly Rob, who is about as loathsome as five generations of this country has ever produced, was going up to her room to maybe get off with her. Had I misread this culture that much?

[*The lights go down and up again on* LIZ *opening the door to* ROB. *She's in her dressing gown and looking very suspicious.*]

LIZ: What did you want?

ROB: Are you going to let me in?

[LIZ *stands back and lets him come in. He closes the door after him and moves across to a chair. He sits down. She follows him, but remains standing. He looks at her. She waits for him to explain the reason for his visit.*]

LIZ: So what is it that you've got to tell me?

ROB: I just wanted to say I'm sorry.

LIZ: About the batteries?

ROB: You did your job perfectly and I stuffed things up.

LIZ: We all make mistakes.

ROB: And I wanted to thank you for making the point to Paul and Kostas that it was an understandable mistake.

LIZ: That's O.K.

ROB: Look, I wouldn't normally barge in at this hour, but I was just sitting in my room when it struck me how bad you must feel. I won't mention names but there was a lot of opposition from some quarters to you taking part in this operation, so it must be doubly galling for you to know that you achieved all that you were asked to achieve and I stuffed it up.

LIZ: [*eyes narrowing*] Who was against me taking part?

ROB: It should be fairly obvious.

LIZ: Kostas?

ROB: [*nods*] Yep.

LIZ: As far as he's concerned women are only good for one thing.

ROB: Absolutely. Note the front desk receptionist.

LIZ: Is he doing it with her?

ROB: You didn't know?

LIZ: The poor little thing in the K-Mart smock?

ROB: After two days sleeping alone Kostas would go to bed with a lump of warm dough.

LIZ: [*tersely*] I can't imagine you were enthusiastic about me being on this operation either.

ROB: I can't say I was, but I didn't go off the deep end like him. And I'm more than willing to admit I made a mistake.

LIZ: He isn't?

ROB: He's still saying it was just a fluke.

LIZ: Just a fluke? See if he says that when I do it again.

ROB: My generation takes women's aspirations seriously. Young blokes like Kostas seem to have reverted to the mindless sexism of the fifties.

LIZ: I'm glad to hear you're taking 'women's aspirations' seriously. I haven't noticed it up to now.

ROB: Liz, sometimes I sense a wall of hostility between us, and I don't think there need be.

LIZ: I'm glad to hear that. I sensed most of the hostility was coming from you.

ROB: I'll be honest. I thought you weren't qualified for the job, but now you've proved you are, all I can say is I'm sorry. Let's mend fences.

LIZ: Sure, but not at eleven at night.

ROB: Why are you so tense?

LIZ: I'm not.

ROB: Not now, in general.

LIZ: In general? Because I'm working with three men, two of whom, until very recently, made it perfectly plain that they thought I was a bimbo.

ROB: Even when you're relaxed you're tense. A woman as beautiful as you are should glide, flow.

LIZ: There's nothing wrong with the way I move.

ROB: Can I show you something?

LIZ: What?

ROB: Just how tense your muscles are? You probably don't realise.

[ROB *gets up and moves towards her. She backs off.*]

LIZ: I'm fine.

ROB: Just let me show you something.

[LIZ *hesitates, then stops retreating.* ROB *goes behind her and grasps the muscles of her shoulders and neck.*]

Can you feel how tense your shoulders are?

LIZ: Yes.

[ROB *steers her to a chair, sits her down and begins massaging her neck from behind.*]

ROB: Loosen up. Relax. I can feel the knots.

[*He continues to massage. His rhythms are sensuous and effective. He's done this before.*]

If these muscles up here are tense, they pull your spine out of line and the muscles down here have to work harder than they should and eventually you'll have recurrent lower back pain which is hell on wheels.

[*He leans her forward and works on her lower back.*]

That's better. I can feel that whole chain relaxing. Can you feel that?

[LIZ *is genuinely responding to the massage by now.*]

LIZ: Yeah that's nice. Really nice. I am tense a lot of the time.

ROB: Honey, you're a coiled spring. Believe me I've watched you.

LIZ: Yeah, well it is a strain when you know you're being put down by everyone.

[ROB *continues to massage her lower back, moving up to her shoulders and down along her arms.*]

ROB: Don't get too paranoid. It's harder for a woman but a man would still have to earn respect if he came in without any background.

LIZ: Kostas came in without any specific training in this area and from what I hear suddenly Paul's smiling ear to ear and the soundtrack is the Hallelujah chorus.

ROB: Plodding cop grooms streetwise wiz kid.

LIZ: And this is the same Kostas who puts the whole operation in jeopardy by rutting himself ragged with the check-in chick.

ROB: And who won't even get reprimanded for doing it.

LIZ: [*responding to the massage*] That's nice. Oh yeah. More there. Harder. That's nice. I was just a coffee maker for six months before Paul let me come up here. And even then they treated me like an idiot.

[*She imitates* PAUL.]

'Don't get him angry. Be patient. Be reasonable. It may need four, five sessions.' I just nodded my head, went in there and did what my instincts told me to do and I had it all in five minutes. I was born for this sort of job. I can run rings around those idiots and there I was for six months making the coffee. And you're trying to tell me women aren't discriminated against?

ROB: Point taken. How's that?

LIZ: [*responding to the massage*] That is really, really good. Where did you learn to do this?

ROB: Where did you learn how to get grafters to spill their guts? Instinct. Some of us have it, some of us don't.

LIZ: I can feel them all unknotting. That's great. You've done this before.

ROB: Many times. And no complaints.

[ROB *moves his hands up her neck and starts caressing her temples.*]

All the muscle groups are connected. The tension transmits itself right up here to the temples.

[*He rubs her temples, her cheeks, her jaw and her neck.*] You get a lot of tension headaches don't you?

LIZ: Yeah.

ROB: [*nods*] I can feel the knotted muscles. Restricts the blood flow. Your brain protests.

LIZ: That is wonderful. That is really wonderful.

ROB: There are fifty-three separate muscles in your face. It takes that many to organise all your facial expressions.

LIZ: Really? Oh that's great. That's really great.

[ROB *lets his hands flow down from her head and neck to her breasts. She lets it happen for a about five seconds and groans with pleasure. Then she suddenly sits upright.*]

[*shaking her head*] Uh huh.

ROB: Lie on the bed. I'll do your legs and thighs.

LIZ: [*shaking head*] Uh Huh. Rob, I'm wonderfully relaxed, you've done a brilliant job. Now I have to sleep.

ROB: I can make you feel ten times better than this.

LIZ: Not tonight. I'm too tired.

ROB: I'll take you to dinner tomorrow night and then I'll get you really relaxed.

LIZ: Sounds great.

[ROB *kisses her. She responds, then steers him towards the door.*]

[*to audience*] Try not to make easy judgements. If you were stuck up in a town whose nightlife could be powered by our four flat batteries, couldn't you have let things drift a little? The truth is some of you would have let them drift a little more. But I knew if I'd've let it go any further the number of people who got to hear about it would cause crowd control problems in your average football stadium. The fact that a man is a total shit doesn't mean he can't excite. One of the cruellest ironies of life is that the most charming men at the restaurant table are often the dullest under the sheets. My most exciting night in bed was spent with a man who the kindest of my friends described as 'gross'. I felt bad about it and made sure I never saw him again, but there you go.

[*The lights fade, then up again in* KOSTAS's *room.* KOSTAS *is sitting up reading. He's agitated. He gets up, moves to the fridge, takes out a beer, takes the cap off, and takes a gulp. He looks at his watch.* ROB *opens the door and enters looking pleased with himself.*]

ROB: Still up.

KOSTAS: I guess you lost your bet?

ROB: Wrong.

KOSTAS: You're back too early.

ROB: She doesn't like guys staying on.

KOSTAS: You did it?

ROB: The thing you've got to realise about women Kostas, is that basically they love it. The species wouldn't've propagated unless they did.

KOSTAS: You did it? With her?

ROB: Look at her face in the morning.

KOSTAS: Bullshit.

ROB: Look at her face in the morning. You'll see a woman who has thrilled to multiple orgasms, and you'll pay me a hundred dollars.

KOSTAS: [*to audience*] I couldn't work out why I was so shattered. What did I care. Bitch. Anyone who'd go to bed with Rob just like that - forget it!
[*to* ROB] So what happens next?

ROB: We'll do it again tomorrow night. And the next. Until we leave.

KOSTAS: And then?

ROB: That's it.

KOSTAS: That's it? Someone as classy as Liz?

ROB: There's no way I'd get involved with her mate. She's poison.

KOSTAS: She's poison? You've just gone and slept with her and she's poison?

ROB: Who are you to be talking. You've just been shagging the poor kid on the front desk. Did you know she was engaged?

KOSTAS: I liked her. I don't make a habit of going to bed with women I hate.

ROB: What is this? Mr Moralist. Mr Greek Orthodox?

KOSTAS: If you think someone is poison you don't go to bed with them. Why is she poison?

ROB: Why? Sit down and I'll tell you.

[KOSTAS *sits himself down and looks at* ROB *defiantly.* ROB *smirks, helps himself to a beer and sits down opposite* KOSTAS, *savouring the moment. The lights fade. They come up at the reception desk.* SHARON, *the front desk girl, stands, waiting.* KOSTAS *goes past. It's the following morning.*]

SHARON: [*bitterly*] You don't even bother to say hello these days.

KOSTAS: Sharon. Sorry I didn't see you there.

SHARON: You couldn't've been looking too hard.

KOSTAS: Sharon, I'm in a hurry.

SHARON: I told Greg.

KOSTAS: You what?

SHARON: What d'you expect? I can just jump into bed with someone else, find out he's a liar, then go back to Greg as if nothing has happened?

KOSTAS: So what did he say?

SHARON: He wants to kill you. I told him you're not worth the effort.

KOSTAS: Sharon, I had no idea my wife was going to come up here - -

SHARON: I had no idea you had a wife. I'm standing here and this woman comes up and says 'I believe my husband is staying here. I'm just checking into his room.' And I think, 'Oh that's nice. Probably the wife of one of those sales reps in the rooms near you', and I say, 'What's his name?' and she smiles and says it's you. Really made my morning.

KOSTAS: Sharon I had no idea she was coming.

SHARON: That makes it better does it? You tell me you're single and that I'm special and fresh and honest and that

you've never felt like this before, and suddenly there she
is, wearing clothes that make me feel like I've just won
Dag of the Year, and all I can do is go away and howl for
two straight days.

KOSTAS: Sharon I meant what I said. You've got a very, very
special quality - -

SHARON: Yeah, I've got big tits and I'm stupid!

KOSTAS: Sharon I wouldn't't've gone near you if my marriage
wasn't as good as over.

SHARON: Oh yeah. Sure. As good as over. That's why she
comes all the way up here to see you.

KOSTAS: We're going to be divorced. She came up here so
we could talk it through.

SHARON: Why couldn't she wait until you got back to the
city?

KOSTAS: Because that's how Liz is.

SHARON: Her name's Sheena.

KOSTAS: Sheena Elizabeth. I call her Liz. [Pause] That's
exactly why our marriage hasn't worked. She can never
wait. Everything has to be settled instantly.

SHARON: [wanting to believe] My sister's like that.

KOSTAS: Everything has to be done according to her timetable.
Everything's got to fit in with her.

SHARON: My sister's like that.

KOSTAS: It's driven me crazy. Our marriage is as good as
over. If you want the absolute truth, I can't stand her.

SHARON: She's prettier than me.

KOSTAS: Sharon, it's the person inside that counts.

SHARON: [sharply] You didn't have to agree so quickly!

KOSTAS: You're both very different.

SHARON: If I spent hours every morning putting on makeup I
could look pretty good too.

KOSTAS: You look great without it.

SHARON: Kostas, when I fall for someone, I fall hard. I fell
for you and I fell hard and when I thought it was all a
pack of lies I seriously thought about killing myself. Did
you know that?

KOSTAS: Sharon, I'm sorry.

SHARON: Well where do I stand now?

KOSTAS: [*edgy*] Sharon, it's been pretty heavy since Sheena arrived. I'm in a bit of a mess.

SHARON: You still love her or something?

KOSTAS: [*sharply*] No!

SHARON: If you hate her and you want a divorce, you should be happy.

KOSTAS: Sharon. We have had a shared history. There have been good moments.

SHARON: She's come here after a reconciliation hasn't she?

KOSTAS: No she hasn't! It's over, but there is some grief.

SHARON: Have you told her about me?

KOSTAS: Sharon it's hardly the time.

SHARON: Not even important enough to rate a mention?

KOSTAS: [*irritation, half real, half fake*] Sharon! What happened between you and me was very very important to me. But it was a mistake to start an affair with you before I'd cleared all this up!

SHARON: Greg tried to kiss me and I just pushed him away. I'm not a trollop Kostas. I can't switch from one man to the next. I've fallen for you Kostas, and I've fallen hard. What am I supposed to do about that?

KOSTAS: When I get my head clear again we can see if it's all still there.

SHARON: No you won't. This is piss off time. I might be stupid but I'm not that stupid.

KOSTAS: Sharon, I just can't think straight now. Can't you understand that?

SHARON: You don't love me do you? You never did. Just have the guts to tell me!

KOSTAS: I like you very much I'm just not sure whether it's love.

SHARON: Yeah, well when you do work it out would you mind telling me so I can work out whether to kill myself or what?
[*The lights fade. They go up again in* PAUL's *room. He's lying on the bed, staring at the ceiling. There is a knock on the door. It's mid morning. Same day.*]

PAUL: It isn't locked.
[*The door opens and* LIZ *comes in.*]

LIZ: Hi. What's happening?

PAUL: We're just waiting for Billy Nottle to reappear.

LIZ: Still no sign.

PAUL: He said he'd ring Kostas.

[PAUL *and* LIZ *look at each other.*]

LIZ: [*to audience*] I flirted, but I honestly didn't plan it to go further. And that's the truth.

PAUL: [*to audience*] She worked on me. I probably read too much into it, but there's no doubt in my mind that she used all the tricks. But let's be a bit more honest. I was waiting for a sign. I'd been waiting for months. I was besotted with the woman. That's why I gave her the job.

[*to* LIZ] There's no future in this unit Liz. The Billy Nottles of this State are as big as we're going to get.

LIZ: It's important enough to get the Billy Nottles.

PAUL: It's not important enough for me. Not in a country with a drug trade that's going out of control and a crime rate that's following it.

LIZ: That's a point.

[*She sits on the bed beside him.*]

PAUL: I'm not sure I can make much difference, but I want to give it a try.

LIZ: Are you going back into the police force?

PAUL: Yeah, but on my terms.

LIZ: Which are?

PAUL: [*shakes head*] You'll think I'm up myself.

LIZ: I think you're the type of guy who *could* do something Paul.

PAUL: I'll go back in if I go as the heir apparent. Otherwise I'll practise law.

LIZ: You want to be number one?

PAUL: The joke who runs the force retires in four years.

LIZ: You'd still be very young.

PAUL: They said I was too young to apply for Inspector and I got it. They said I was too young to apply for this job and I got it.

LIZ: You know what I like about you?

PAUL: What?

LIZ: You're sure of yourself. It borders on arrogance.

PAUL: Arrogance? No one's ever accused me of that before.

LIZ: [*lays a hand on his arm*] I like it. I sometimes call myself
a feminist, so I know I shouldn't, but I find men who have
a touch of arrogance very attractive.

PAUL: Women don't like wimps.

LIZ: [*nods*] I think it's biological. Maybe we're looking for
men who can look after us when we're pregnant and
vulnerable. It's very confusing.

PAUL: So what do you do about it?

LIZ: I live like a Nun.

PAUL: You shouldn't.

LIZ: I don't want to.

PAUL: What do you want?

LIZ: I want a relationship with a man I love and admire.

PAUL: Marriage. Kids?

LIZ: Eventually. But first I want to do something with my
life.

PAUL: Like what?

LIZ: Like this. If I help catch a few Billy Nottles I'll feel as
if I've achieved something.

PAUL: You will have.

LIZ: This has been a very special time in my life Paul. You're
the first person who's really given me a chance. I just hope
I'm managing.

PAUL: You're doing brilliantly.

[LIZ *and* PAUL *stare at each other.*]

LIZ: [*to audience*] I think I said 'You're arrogant but I love
it.' I can't remember. If I did I shouldn't have. It's lethal.
Every guy is either arrogant or would like to think he is.
When you present it as a virtue they go wild. As a woman
you've got to come to terms fairly early with the fact that
your average male is a different species. Poor grasp of
language, minimal interest in relationships, little
appreciation of nature, beauty, complexity - little capacity
for compassion. I'm not saying that they're robots, but then
again I'm not saying that they're not. You don't necessarily
agree? A sweeping generalisation? [*She shrugs.*] Listen to
them when they talk. Who won, who lost. Who's on the
way up, who's on the way down. Who broke the rules and
who's going to pay. But unless you're a lesbian and I'm

not, you're stuck with them. Worse than that, actively
attracted. Worse than that, in my case, attracted to the ones
with status and power. But this was different. Here I was
finding myself genuinely attracted to someone who was
genuinely decent and, dare I say it. Nice.
[*to* PAUL] Paul, could you find some reason why we have
to have dinner together tonight?

PAUL: Do we need a reason?

LIZ: Rob. He won't leave me alone.

PAUL: Rob?

LIZ: He walked into my room last night and made it pretty
obvious what he was after.

PAUL: [*angry*] The sooner I get rid of that prick the better.

LIZ: Please don't tell him I said anything. I just wanted you
to know.

PAUL: [*angry*] I'll flatten him. What does he think? You're
up here for his amusement?

LIZ: He obviously thinks the opportunity's too good to miss,
but please don't say I said anything. Please.

PAUL: [*anger and passion bursting out*] What does he think?
You're some kind of casual lay or something? He's got a
wife and kids! Jesus!
[*He sits down, trying to control his passion.*]
You shouldn't have to put up with it.

LIZ: He marched in there as if he was doing me a big favour.
I couldn't believe his attitude. I'm here as a professional
member of this unit, not a recreational facility. I got so
angry. I was shaking when he left.

PAUL: I can't believe guys like that. You're a fantastic woman.
If I wasn't married I'd be down on my knees begging you
to put me on your list of possibles. To just consider me.
[LIZ *stares at him as if this was the last thing she
expected to hear.* PAUL *looks at her.*]
I'm sorry. I wasn't ever going to say that.

LIZ: [*staring at him, still feigning surprise*] Paul. I had no
idea that you felt - -

PAUL: [*it comes pouring out*] I can't believe that some crud
like Rob can - -
[*He can't find the words*]

I miss you over the weekends. That's how bad it gets. I can't concentrate on the family. I can't wait to get back and see you again on Monday.

LIZ: [to audience] His declaration of love came out in language you wouldn't describe as poetic. 'I can't live without you', things like that, but it was unexpectedly passionate. Passionate enough to get me unexpectedly excited. And also a little alarmed. I was honest enough with myself even back then to know that I wasn't going to end up as second wife of the Chief of Police. With four visiting rug rats pre-programmed by wife number one to radiate hostility. I had to abort the whole thing.

[LIZ turns back to PAUL and stares at him.]

Paul, if you weren't married, you wouldn't have to be on your knees. You'd be right at the top of my list - -

[to audience] But whatever I said he misinterpreted. He kissed me with enormous passion. Then he kissed me again more gently. And he's a very attractive man. And even though all the warning bells were ringing, I couldn't stop myself. Within minutes, if we're talking Mills and Boon, I felt the hard tense throb of his passion. Often when I'm involved with someone a secret nickname comes tumbling out of my unconscious. Paul became indelibly imprinted on my mind as 'Rocket.'

PAUL: [to audience] When we made love it was explosive. This is going to sound dumb, but it was as if our bodies had been waiting for each other for a lifetime. If she was honest Liz would've admitted this too.

LIZ: [to audience] You've got to believe, 'Rocket' notwithstanding, I was genuinely fond of Paul. I really liked him. It was a flirtation that got out of hand.

[The lights fade and go up in KOSTAS's room. There is a knock at the door. PAUL walks in. He is trying hard to control a combination of elation and anxiety. KOSTAS doesn't notice. It's mid afternoon.]

KOSTAS: Where've you been all the afternoon? I phone up and you're engaged or your phone's off the hook, and I go round and bash on your door and no one's there.

PAUL: I've been out.

KOSTAS: Billy Nottle's back. I'm trying to get hold of him.

PAUL: Great.

KOSTAS: I hope Liz bloody does what she's told this time and doesn't antagonise him.

PAUL: Just leave it to her instincts. She'll be fine.

[KOSTAS *looks at him sharply. There's something about* PAUL's *enthusiasm for* LIZ *which alerts him.*]

KOSTAS: Have you - -

PAUL: Have I what?

KOSTAS: It's happened, hasn't it?

PAUL: What?

KOSTAS: You and Liz?

[PAUL *looks at him. Then nods.*]

PAUL: I've got to have her mate. When I talk to her it's like I've never talked to anyone else in my life. She understands me better than I understand myself. She knows what I'm going to say before I've said it.

KOSTAS: [*sourly*] You know why? You're totally fucking predictable.

PAUL: [*angrily*] Mate, we've only got one bloody life.

KOSTAS: Thank God. I couldn't bear two stuff ups.

PAUL: This isn't just a weekend romance - mate, we're only on this earth once - -

KOSTAS: You said that.

PAUL: We are, so it's crazy not to go after something better than mere existence.

KOSTAS: Mere existence? Helen and the kids would be really pleased to hear themselves described as mere existence.

PAUL: You know what I mean.

KOSTAS: No, I don't know what you mean. I think you're a fucking idiot!

PAUL: Mate, I got Helen pregnant when I was nineteen. I married her because I thought that's what you had to do, and she's a good person and a good wife and I love my kids, but this is like - -

KOSTAS: Like you're experiencing life for the first time, like you're in a new dimension, like a canary is singing in your nostril?

PAUL: Will you stop being so bloody cynical!

KOSTAS: Mate, snap out of it before you get yourself hurt! She's playing with you.

[PAUL *grabs him by the lapels and shoves him up against the wall.*]

PAUL: You've been slagging her since she came to this unit.

KOSTAS: O.K. You don't want to listen. Go ahead. Ruin your life.

[*Shaking himself free suddenly and violently*]

And don't fucking manhandle me. You're not back in the vice squad now!

[PAUL *glares at him.* KOSTAS *maintains the gaze.*]

PAUL: This is serious mate. The most serious thing that's ever happened to me in my life.

KOSTAS: Rob went up to her room last night. In half an hour he had her in bed.

PAUL: You believe him?

KOSTAS: I heard him ring her. I saw him go.

PAUL: She told me. He went to her room and tried it on and she got mad as hell and told him to get out!

KOSTAS: She took a long time to get mad mate. I was here when he left, I was here when he got back.

PAUL: You really believe she'd go to bed with Rob?

KOSTAS: What am I supposed to think? He was gone for an hour or more.

PAUL: Mate, there's no way Rob got her to bed. He's a scumbag and a bullshit artist and it doesn't say much for your ability to see through people if you believe what he says.

KOSTAS: So why was he there so long?

PAUL: Well he's not going to come straight back down and tell you he failed is he? Use your bloody head!

KOSTAS: Even if she didn't do anything with Rob she's got another guy.

[PAUL *stares at him.*]

PAUL: How do you know that?

KOSTAS: She's got a guy. Big time finance broker. He's just left his family for her. Rob plays golf with a guy who works with him.

PAUL: I wouldn't believe a word that turd said.

KOSTAS: It's true. He drives a black Porsche, drinks Dom Perignon - that's her scene mate. She's out of our league.
[*To audience*]
I think I said something like 'She's out of our league.' Not 'She's out of your league.' 'She's out of our league.' The news of her big time lover had hit me almost as hard as it had hit Paul. At that time I wasn't admitting to myself why.
[PAUL *looks stricken.*]
Sorry mate. I had to tell you before the damage got worse. [*Pause*] You've got a great wife and great kids. What were you going to do? Leave them and let 'em grow up without a cent to their name?

PAUL: I love her Kostas. What the hell am I supposed to do about this.

KOSTAS: It goes in a few days mate. Come on. It's happened to you before.

PAUL: It hasn't happened before and it's not going to go in a few days.

KOSTAS: Then start learning to sing the blues man. Start learning to sing the blues.
[*To audience*]
But what I didn't say is 'I'll probably join you.'

PAUL: [*to audience*] My first impulse was to go and confront her, then I pulled back. I was scared that the story was true and the last thing I wanted to hear right then was the truth.
[PAUL *leaves the stage,* KOSTAS *remains.* LIZ *joins him.*]

LIZ: [*to audience*] I'm feeling really guilty about a word I used. Robot. I don't want half of you to go out to interval thinking 'She thinks we're Robots.' It was just one of those half truths or quarter truths you say when you're trying to be clever. Men can be terrific. Chivalrous, fair, logical, calm. There was another man, and he did drive a black Porsche, and he had just left his wife and kids. But please suspend judgement until the second half. I'm not claiming it exonerates me, but I pay for my sins.

KOSTAS: [*overhearing*] You pay for your sins? Are you kidding?

LIZ: I'm forced to face up to things.

KOSTAS: But do you suffer? Honestly? Do you really suffer?

LIZ: Not as much as you'd like me to obviously, but yes, I suffer.

KOSTAS: I hope you never have to really suffer. That's all I can say.

LIZ: [to audience] Maybe I get off too easily. It didn't feel easy to me.

[LIZ leaves with an angry backward glance at KOSTAS.]

KOSTAS: [to audience] I'm the one that suffers. Not her.

[KOSTAS leaves. ROB steps forward as he watches LIZ and KOSTAS go.]

ROB: [to audience] She played with me in the first act. Loved the massage, was itching to get laid, but didn't have the guts to see it through. Don't worry. I'm persistent. Go and have a drink and come back and you'll see what I mean. Interval.

[The lights fade.]

INTERVAL

ACT TWO

The lights fade up. LIZ *is lying on the bed reading in her bathrobe. There is a knock at the door. It's evening.*

LIZ: Come in.
    [ROB *comes in.*]
    Hi.
ROB: You're tense again.
LIZ: I'm not tense again. I'm perfectly relaxed.
ROB: Ready for Billy Nottle tomorrow?
LIZ: [*alert*] Is he back?
ROB: Kostas hasn't told you?
LIZ: No.
ROB: Won't they be using you to try and get Nottle to spill his guts again?
LIZ: [*tense*] That was the plan.
ROB: Maybe Kostas thinks he can do it himself.
LIZ: How long has he known? That Nottle was back.
ROB: He told me this morning.
LIZ: [*angry*] That's great!
    [*She picks up the phone and dials.* ROB *shakes his head.*]
ROB: They're down in the bar.
LIZ: I haven't heard one bloody word!
ROB: Strange.
LIZ: [*angry*] I can't believe this! I get them everything they need in five minutes and they're not going to use me this time?
ROB: They probably are, but it's odd Kostas hasn't told you. Mind you he's still really pissed off that you got the stuff out of Nottle and he couldn't.
LIZ: If I'd failed, fair enough, but it's just so typical of insecure little schmucks like Kostas to do something like this.
ROB: He's probably just letting you sweat a while.
LIZ: Kostas and Paul are in the bar now? [ROB *nods.*] I should be there !
    [*She gets up and moves to the door, then comes back.*]
    Well don't you think I should be there?

ROB: Absolutely, so should I, but we never get invited to the inner cabinet.

LIZ: Men like that really piss me off !

ROB: It's really important to you, this, isn't it?

LIZ: Why shouldn't it be?

ROB: Someone like you doesn't have to worry about catching little crooks like Billy Nottle.

LIZ: Someone like me? What do you mean, someone like me?

ROB: You're classy. You could - -

LIZ: I could what?

ROB: You could be anything you wanted.

LIZ: Could I? You tell me what I could be?

ROB: The wife of some rich guy.

LIZ: That's the last thing I want to be!

ROB: What do you want?

LIZ: I want to be good at something.

ROB: You want to be good at something.

LIZ: Most people want to be good at something. Is that so strange?

ROB: No.

LIZ: I have this fantasy. At least once a day. The phone is jammed with people trying to get through to me. 'Hey Liz, we've got this problem, do you think you can handle it', and I say 'Yeah, I can handle it. Sure I can handle it.'

ROB: Phone jammed with people with problems? Fantasy? That's a nightmare.

LIZ: Not to me.

ROB: My idea of a great morning is when the phone doesn't ring at all.

LIZ: I'd kill for the respect you get when you can do something well. My father can operate on someone and save their hearing. You can be as cynical as you like, but that's something. I just want to be able to do something and do it well.

ROB: Did you ever want to be a doctor?

LIZ: Yeah. But I didn't get anywhere near the marks needed to get in. I scraped into arts and failed that. Mainly because I wasn't interested but I still failed.

   [*She looks at the door, deciding whether to go.*]

Maybe I'm not going to make a permanent career out of duping the Billy Nottles of the world, but I did it, and I did it brilliantly, and they've got no right to stop me trying again!

[*She's angry and upset.*]

I can't go down there and face them now or I'll just scream. And they'll say hysterical woman, and that'll be that.

ROB: Calm down. Sit here.

[ROB *guides her to a chair and sits her down. He begins to rub her neck.*]

Tense. You are really tense.

LIZ: Just don't think you're going to get me to bed. I've had enough of that sort of pressure already.

ROB: Who, Kostas?

LIZ: No.

ROB: Who?

LIZ: What do you guys think? That I'm just up here for your sexual convenience? You're all a bit bored so you head for me?

ROB: Paul?

LIZ: You trust someone, and ten minutes later they're stabbing you in the back.

ROB: Did Paul and you -

LIZ: Paul and I have done nothing.

ROB: Paul's not your speed.

LIZ: Paul's not the issue.

ROB: Did he really put the hard word on?

LIZ: Don't make out that's not what you're about either.

ROB: Me? Married man. Father of two.

LIZ: Go and pay for a prostitute if you're all that desperate.

ROB: Liz, you're not talking to Kostas. I don't buy sex. I make love.

LIZ: Not to me. Not tonight.

[ROB *continues stroking her. She responds to the sensuality.*]

ROB: How's that?

LIZ: Men are bastards! Absolute bastards!

[ROB *strokes her forehead.*]

ROB: Hey, no frowning. Loosen up. Think of something relaxing. Making love to a sensitive and caring man.

LIZ: If those two bastards don't use me I am going to throw a megatantrum in the foyer.

ROB: Come over here, lie down, and let me work on your back.

[LIZ *looks at him doubtfully, but lets herself be led over to the bed. She lies face down.*]

LIZ: If you lay one finger anyplace you shouldn't, you're dead.

[ROB *begins massaging her back with long sensuous movements.*]

ROB: Nice?

LIZ: Mmm. That's really nice.

[ROB *moves his area of massage down to her buttocks.*]
No Rob. Back.

ROB: Back.

[ROB *rubs her back and* LIZ *starts emitting low groans of contentment.*]

ROB: You want to be something useful?

LIZ: Yeah.

ROB: Missionary. I don't know why that position gets such derision. I find it one of the more caring configurations.

LIZ: I've thought of being a foreign aid worker.

ROB: Helping to dig the village pump in Bangladesh?

LIZ: [*loss of interest*] Yeah.

ROB: Great idea. You'd get respect, love, everything you need.

LIZ: [*unenthusiastic*] Yeah.

ROB: Except the respect of a few impoverished Bangladeshis is not quite what you're after, correct?

LIZ: You're really smart aren't you?

ROB: [*nods*] I'm also great in bed.

LIZ: I'm going to have to take your word for that. Just keep rubbing.

[*She moans in pleasure as he pounds the small of her back. There's a cursory knock at the door and* PAUL *enters. He stares at* ROB *and* LIZ.]
Hi.

PAUL: Hi.

ROB: Hi.

LIZ: [*tersely*] So what's happening?
PAUL: What's happening?
LIZ: Billy Nottle's back I believe?
PAUL: Yeah.
LIZ: So what's happening?
PAUL: About what?
LIZ: About the operation tomorrow? Am I involved?
PAUL: We'll talk in the morning.
LIZ: Am I involved?
PAUL: Of course.
LIZ: Why didn't you tell me he was back?
    [PAUL *is fighting to restrain his bewilderment at her attitude.*]
PAUL: It isn't that urgent.
LIZ: Rob said you and Kostas were making plans in the bar.
PAUL: No we weren't.
ROB: [*to* PAUL] I thought you and I weren't supposed to be seen with Kostas or Liz in public?
PAUL: People strike up casual conversations in bars. Could I see you alone for a minute Liz?
ROB: Leave her alone Paul.
PAUL: What?
ROB: Leave her alone. She's not here just as some kind of convenience.
PAUL: Get out of here.
ROB: [*as he goes*] I mean it mate. Just leave her alone.
    [PAUL *stares at him, then at* LIZ.]
PAUL: What the hell's going on?
LIZ: I let him rub my back. He's inflated that into thinking he owns me.
PAUL: Why do you let him rub your back?
LIZ: Because he pesters me every hour of the day and if I'm totally rude to him it virtually means we can't work together. Listen what's going on about tomorrow?
PAUL: We'll talk about it in the morning. Nottle's not coming until the afternoon.
LIZ: Shouldn't we be discussing how we're going to tackle it now?

PAUL: [*annoyed*] Will you leave the tactics to me! Why the hell do you have to be so friendly with Rob?

LIZ: [*biting back*] I told you.

PAUL: [*passionately*] Liz, when you walk out a door, life as good as stops for me until you come in another one. If I'm making a fool of myself for Christ's sake tell me.

LIZ: Of course you're not making a fool of yourself.

PAUL: Liz, what's happened between us is probably the most important thing that's ever happened to me in my entire life! If it doesn't mean that to you then tell me!

LIZ: [*to audience*] I can remember Paul getting enormously passionate. I think he said I was the most important thing in his life. It was very flattering but the warning bells were ringing again.

[*to* PAUL] Paul, I feel the same - -

PAUL: So why are you letting that creep massage you?

LIZ: Paul, that's all he was doing.

PAUL: And why didn't you tell me you've got some other guy!

LIZ: There's someone I was interested in. I'm not any longer.

PAUL: You said you've been living like a Nun.

LIZ: I have. Virtually.

PAUL: Liz, as far as I'm concerned we're not playing footsies any more. It's all or nothing.

[PAUL *stares at her. She stares back at him.*]

LIZ: [*to audience*] He said 'This is for real kid' or something corny like that but with such passion. The drama of it was electric. Suddenly we were making love again. He had the energy of a madman. The more I shrieked in terror, the more he thought I was enjoying it. No, I'm being cynical again. It was exciting.

PAUL: [*to audience*] The second time we made love was the high point of my life.

[*Countering apparent scepticism*]

No, I'm serious. Everything seemed to come together and sweep away any doubts about love and commitment. If Liz was honest, she'd admit that too.

[*The lights fade and go up again on* LIZ's *room. It's morning. She's alone on the bed, sleeping. The phone is off the hook. There is a knock on the door.*]

LIZ: [*pulling her gown around her*] Who is it?

SHARON: [*Voice only*] Front desk.

[LIZ *goes across to the door and opens it.* SHARON *is standing there with a sealed envelope in her hand.*]

Message for your husband.

LIZ: He's gone. I'll take it.

SHARON: I don't suppose he's told you.

LIZ: About what?

SHARON: About him and me.

LIZ: No he hasn't.

SHARON: You're doing the right thing.

LIZ: What?

SHARON: Divorcing him.

LIZ: Did he tell you I was divorcing him?

SHARON: Yeah, he did.

LIZ: What's your name?

SHARON: Sharon.

LIZ: Sharon, I'm not divorcing him. Did he tell you that?

SHARON: Yeah, he did. He said you came up here to talk it through.

LIZ: I came up here to finalise a joint business venture we're establishing.

SHARON: [*shocked*] I'm sorry I shouldn't't've said anything.

LIZ: Sharon, you're not the first and you won't be the last. If you're married to someone like my husband you realise it's part of the deal.

SHARON: You just accept it?

LIZ: [*shrugs*] He's good at dinner parties, and he's good in bed. As I'm sure you've noticed.

SHARON: You just accept it?

LIZ: If I get rid of him the next one would be just as bad.

SHARON: Whatever happened to love!

LIZ: Love is something they sing about in pop songs.

SHARON: Love is not something they sing about in pop songs! Love is something that happens!

SHARON: [*very upset*] How can you talk like that! If there wasn't love what would be the point of staying alive?

LIZ: Try money, power, status and revenge.

[SHARON *stares at her, shocked.*]

[*to audience*] I can remember being pretty awful to the little receptionist. I thought she might learn something about men if I played it tough. [*Pause.*] I think at some deeper level I was pissed off with her because she'd slept with Kostas. But at that stage I wasn't admitting to myself that such a thing could be upsetting.

[KOSTAS *walks up to the open door. He looks at* LIZ *and at* SHARON.]

Message for you dear.

[*She hands him the envelope.* KOSTAS *takes it and begins to open it. He looks at* SHARON *who suddenly lets fly.*]

SHARON: I think that you two are two of the - - lowest - -

[*Words fail her. She turns to the audience.*]

[*to audience*] I remember being so full of anger at the pair of them that I felt I had to do something. My first thought was suicide, but I thought that that wouldn't cause them any more than half an hour's guilt. My life was worth more than that.

[SHARON *storms away.* KOSTAS *watches her go, shrugs, then reads the note.*]

LIZ: She's really, really upset. I hope you realise that?

KOSTAS: Yeah, I feel bad.

LIZ: [*sarcastically, echoing his pre-interval line*] But do you suffer? Honestly? Do you really suffer?

KOSTAS: I do feel bad, but she'll be O.K. Life goes on.

LIZ: Life goes on. You've just broken some poor young kid's heart, do you realise that?

KOSTAS: [*referring to the note*] Just Nottle asking me to ring him. I already have. [*Looks at* LIZ] He won't see you.

LIZ: What did he say?

KOSTAS: He said he'd see me but not you.

[LIZ *looks at him.*]?

You got what we wanted last time, but you pissed him off so much he won't see you again.

LIZ: I could still barge in - -

KOSTAS: It wouldn't work this time.

LIZ: I won't tackle it the same way! Give me credit for some intelligence.

KOSTAS: We can't risk it.

LIZ: How are you going to get him to say anything. You couldn't last time.

KOSTAS: That's my problem.

LIZ: It's everybody's problem.

KOSTAS: He just won't see you. That's it. It took me all my powers of persuasion to get him to come and see me.

LIZ: [angry] Well that's it for me then. What do I do? Just sit in my room?

KOSTAS: [as he goes] Do what you like. Just stay clear of Billy Nottle.

[LIZ stands there. Angry and frustrated. The lights go up on KOSTAS's room. There's a knock at the door. Mid morning.]

Come in.

[BILLY comes in. He nods at KOSTAS and shows him a sheet of paper.]

This is where you want the money left?

[BILLY nods and starts to tear up the piece of paper.]

Hang on. Give me a second.

[BILLY shows him the paper again. KOSTAS starts to memorise, then suddenly lunges and grabs the pad. BILLY tries to wrench it back, but KOSTAS wins the struggle.]

Billy. Do you want the bad news or the good news?

[BILLY stares at him.]

The bad news is that you're going to jail. The good news is that it'll probably only be for ten years or so.

[BILLY stares at him.]

Sorry to spring this on you old mate, but my real name is Kostas and I'm with the Task Force against Corruption, and my lovely wife Sheena isn't my lovely wife, and we've got all the things you said to her last week on tape and they've been checked with the public prosecutor's office and they're more than enough to get you on a charge of conspiracy to misuse a public office. What have you got to say to that?

BILLY: Is this a joke?

KOSTAS: No Billy, you're in deep shit.

BILLY: I knew there was something fishy about you two!

KOSTAS: Then why did you agree to take our fifty thousand?

BILLY: Because I'm bloody stupid!

KOSTAS: Greedy, Billy.

BILLY: [angry] Why don't you catch the real crims! The most I've ever made out of this is a couple of thousand bucks a go. Yours was going to be the big one!
[to audience] That wasn't strictly true. Fifty thousand was pretty standard for big developments, but I wasn't about to tell him that.

KOSTAS: Did it ever occur to you that you weren't supposed to use your position on the council to organise kickbacks, Mr Nottle?

BILLY: I've only done what plenty of other bastards around the country are doing. Why the hell are you picking on me?

KOSTAS: Thank you Mr Nottle. We didn't have you on tape last time but we have now.
[KOSTAS takes a tape recorder out of his pocket and plays it back. We hear BILLY's voice say, 'I've only done what plenty of other bastards around the State are doing.']
That, together with this drop address in your own handwriting means you're well and truly stuffed Billy.

BILLY: How much?

KOSTAS: How much?

BILLY: How much for that tape?

KOSTAS: Billy, you're getting yourself in deeper.

BILLY: Fifty thousand cash. I'm serious.
[KOSTAS looks at him and frowns. The lights dim. They come up again in KOSTAS's room. ROB is standing next to him. Mid morning.]

ROB: Fifty thousand. [He whistles, then pauses.] Tempting isn't it?

KOSTAS: It's not as if we've just caught the Mr Big of organised crime.

ROB: Paul's been on the take.
[KOSTAS looks at him, surprised.]

When he was in the vice squad. Took money for over a
year.

KOSTAS: What are you saying? Split three ways?

ROB: [thinks then shakes head] He wouldn't be in it these
days.

KOSTAS: What d'you reckon?

ROB: Twenty five thousand each? I reckon we go for it.

KOSTAS: [to audience] It all seemed so easy. Twenty five
thousand right there, and all you had to do was reach.

`[The lights fade and go up. PAUL is now with ROB and
KOSTAS.]

PAUL: You couldn't get him to say a word?

KOSTAS: Nothing. He gave a drop address, but we'd only catch
one of the messenger boys.

PAUL: You pretended we had that tape of him and Liz?

KOSTAS: [uneasy] He didn't buy it. He just didn't buy it.

PAUL: It's been a great operation, hasn't it?

[The lights come up. We're in PAUL's room. He's looking
shocked at what he's hearing from ROB.]

ROB: He offered me half. Twenty five thousand.

PAUL: He's got Nottle on tape?

ROB: Everything we need. I listened to it.

PAUL: Jesus!

ROB: I told him not to be such a stupid young arsehole, but
he kept on and on. If we let him off with a reprimand,
he'll do it again next time.

PAUL: [shakes his head] How could he be so stupid?

ROB: We've got to nail him Paul. I know it's a shit thing to
have to do, but corruption in the Task Force against
Corruption is difficult to justify.

PAUL: Just let me think this through for a few hours Rob.
[to audience] Kostas? I couldn't believe it. He's not that
stupid. Get him on this and he's in jail for the next five
or ten years. I couldn't do it. He was like a younger brother.
But I was in a bind. Rob had reported him.
[The lights go down and go up again in LIZ's room. It's
afternoon. She's sitting there looking depressed. There's a
knock on her door. She calls out for the person outside
to come in. He does. It's someone we've never seen

before. STEVEN, *a man in his forties. He's a handsome man who's kept himself in shape, and he's not looking happy.* LIZ *is startled to see him.*]

LIZ: Steven? What are you doing here?

STEVEN: We have to have it out Liz. Once and for all.

LIZ: Steven I'm working. I'm on an operation.

STEVEN: Yeah, well I'm going crazy and I've got to have some answers!

LIZ: How did you find me?

STEVEN: I rang the phone number.

LIZ: You were only supposed to phone me if there was an emergency.

STEVEN: Liz, this is an emergency. I can't take it any more. My wife hates me, my kids won't speak to me, and I've been stuck in a crummy little flat for nearly six months waiting for you to make up your mind about whether we can live together!

LIZ: Steven I can't think about this now! I'm working! We're about to crack one of the biggest scams in the history of this state, and I'm the linchpin of the whole operation!

STEVEN: Just tell me. I walked out on my wife and kids for you! I wrecked a family!

LIZ: It was your decision.

STEVEN: It was my decision. It was my decision, sure, based on the fact that we were both supposed to love each other desperately! And five months later we still don't even live together!

LIZ: We're lovers Steven! That's all I ever promised we'd be!

STEVEN: I see you one or two nights a week if I'm lucky. What kind of commitment is that?

LIZ: Steven, I always made it clear that I thought living together is a very very final commitment, and that I had to be sure.

STEVEN: You said your flat wasn't big enough for two, so we'd live apart until we found the right place for us.

LIZ: If it felt right.

STEVEN: Is it ever going to feel right?

LIZ: Not if you track me down and yell at me when I'm working! Imagine if I burst into your office and stared yelling at you!

STEVEN: Is it ever going to feel right, or have I just busted my marriage and destroyed my kids lives for nothing?

LIZ: [angry] Hey, don't pull that one on me! You told me you couldn't stand your wife. That living with her was like sharing your life with a anorexic Anaconda. And that you were sure your kids would always love you no matter what.

STEVEN: The little bastards won't even talk to me on the fucking phone!

LIZ: Maybe you misjudged something, right? Maybe it's not me that's to blame!

STEVEN: Liz, I can't live without you. I sit there for hours waiting for the phone to ring. And then yesterday I hear stories about this other guy.

LIZ: [startled] What other guy?

STEVEN: Some stockbroker who drives a black Porsche.

LIZ: [flustered] Rick is just a friend.

STEVEN: Then why has he just left his wife and kids?

LIZ: [to audience] When Steven arrived I can remember looking at him and thinking 'How could I have ever found this man attractive?' But when it all started I did. I didn't 'lure' him away from his family like some - - siren. When it happened we were at that magic stage in an affair where you are literally blind to the other's faults. His decisiveness was soon to turn to bullying, his wit to heavy-handed sarcasm, and his precision to an obsession with details, but that was later. If love doesn't last, who's to blame?

STEVEN: [to LIZ] Why has he left his wife and kids?

LIZ: [flustered] You'd have to ask him.

STEVEN: You're having an affair with him aren't you? I've known there's somebody else for weeks!

LIZ: Steven, something's happened to us. The magic isn't there any more.

STEVEN: It is for me.

LIZ: [angry] I can't fake it, Steven.

STEVEN: [angry] So my marriage is wrecked, my children are wrecked and it's all been for nothing!

LIZ: Steven, you took a gamble. I'm sorry about your family, but you made the choice.

STEVEN: What's happened to all our plans? All over? Finished?

LIZ: [*to audience*] Steven had worked out the whole rest of our life. He'd made a lot of money in real estate during the housing boom, and he didn't have to work again. The second half of his life was to be devoted to his cultural education. I was to be his live-in cultural tutor. We were to live in a farmhouse in Bordeaux or Tuscany, learn French, or Italian and read all the novels I thought we should read, and go to New York and London each year to see all the plays and films I thought we should see. I was qualified for the job. I am the sort of person who makes sure I know where the cutting edge of artistic fashion is, and wants to be thought of as being there, but to be truthful, my favourite film was *Raiders of the Lost Ark*.

STEVEN: [*to* LIZ] What about our plans?

LIZ: Steven, they were your plans. I wasn't even consulted.

STEVEN: We talked for hours and hours.

LIZ: Steven, you talked for hours and hours. I have to do something with my life that isn't just tagging along with you.

STEVEN: I can't believe this. If you're telling me that everything's over I might just as well be dead.

[STEVEN *stands there looking stricken.*]

LIZ: [*to audience*] I tried to tell him the truth, but he looked so miserable and helpless that I was suddenly overwhelmed with guilt and I remembered the days when we were in love and I cried, and I took him in my arms and said that the thing with Nick had happened, yes, and he had left his wife and kids, yes, but I hadn't made him any promises, and I was very very confused myself, which was true, and could he please go and book himself into another motel, so we could just think this all through. After he left, I sat there, depressed and overwhelmed. It had all got out of hand. I needed to talk to someone.

[*Lights go down and up in* KOSTAS's *room. Evening. He's sitting there thinking when there's a knock at the door. He calls out for the person to come in and* LIZ *enters.*]

Hi.

KOSTAS: Hi.

LIZ: Could I ask your opinion about something?

KOSTAS: Sure. What?

LIZ: [*she sits down*] Me.

KOSTAS: You?

LIZ: They say if you want to know the truth about yourself go and ask your harshest critic.

KOSTAS: Am I your harshest critic?

LIZ: You'll do. What's the worst thing you've ever heard said about me? Be honest.

KOSTAS: [*thinks*] That you're poison. [*Thinks again*] No wait a minute - -

LIZ: I'm poison?

KOSTAS: You play with guys. It's a sport to you.

LIZ: Kostas, that's not true!

KOSTAS: Men are supposed to chase women, but most guys won't put their ego on the line until they get the signs and you give all the signs.

LIZ: That's like saying women only get raped because they ask for it.

KOSTAS: You give the signs. You've been giving them to Paul for months, and now you've got him, you don't want him any more.

LIZ: [*shaking head*] No.

KOSTAS: You want the truth? The truth is you're poison.

LIZ: What about you? Seducing anything you can lay your hands on? Have you any idea of the agony that poor little receptionist is going through?

KOSTAS: O.K. I'm poison too. I seduce, you seduce. We're both predators.

LIZ: I'm not a predator. I fall for these guys. I really fall.

KOSTAS: Come on. They're conquests. Face up to yourself before you do any more harm.

LIZ: I'm not a predator. I fall in love.

KOSTAS: Liz, you fall in love every time you step in front of a mirror. That's the start and finish of it.

LIZ: If we're talking narcissism, you're the only man I know who keeps twenty signed photos of himself in his wallet.

KOSTAS: Have you got the faintest idea of what it's like to be in a family where your father's gone off with some other woman?

LIZ: I didn't - -

KOSTAS: I'll tell you because I lived in one. It fucks you in the head, that's what it does. It makes you hate your Dad for being a bastard and hate your Mum for not being able to hold onto him and hate yourself for not being 'lovable' enough for your Dad to want to stay in the first place. And it makes you poor. And it makes you think marriage is worth shit, and it makes you hate kids whose parents didn't split up - all in all it's a monster fuck up, it isn't nice, the effects last for ever, and you should be forced to live in a fucked up family like mine was for a year just to see how it feels, because if you did you wouldn't go near a married man ever again!

LIZ: I didn't ask them to leave their precious families!

KOSTAS: Them? Paul's just one of many?

LIZ: Paul won't leave his family. I won't let him.

KOSTAS: You won't be able to stop him. He's off his skull about you.

LIZ: Paul isn't the problem. There's another one here.

KOSTAS: Another one? Another husband? Who's left his wife?
    [LIZ nods.]
    Here? Here in this motel?

LIZ: In this town. He's not meant to be here.

KOSTAS: Mr Black Porsche?

LIZ: How did you know that?

KOSTAS: Mr Black Porsche?

LIZ: [shamefaced] Another one.

KOSTAS: [incredulous] Another one? You're poison. Face up to it, you're poison!

LIZ: [upset, emotional] O.K. I give all the signs. I give all the signs. And they fall for me. And I love it. I love the excitement. I love the drama. Ever since I was fifteen I've

never had less than two or three guys chasing me, and they
never know about each other, and they always think they're
the only one. I guess that makes me poison. [*Pause*] You
know what? The day after Steven left his family, I started
looking for a new guy. I tried to stop myself doing it, but
this edgy thing builds up inside me, and off I go again.
It's like being an addict. [*Pause*] I'm a conquest junkie.
And it's got out of hand.

KOSTAS: I had to go to the Philippines last year. Manila. Ten
dollars buys you a beautiful young girl. Sixteen, seventeen.
They have to do it. They come in from the villages and
it's either that or starvation. So you know if you go into
those bars it's total exploitation. Total. I had a different
one every night for two weeks. Do you think I felt guilty?

LIZ: No.

KOSTAS: How did you guess? No, I didn't feel guilty. Just
like I don't feel guilty about Sharon. I got back to my hotel
room one night and stood there looking out of the window,
and I shouted out with joy. A kind of animal shout of joy.
Couldn't stop it. Just came tumbling out. Why?

LIZ: Because you had a different girl a night for two weeks.

KOSTAS: [*nods*] Because I got my dick into fourteen different
women in less time than it takes to get a kiss out of your
average Greek princess. You want to know the awful truth
about men. I just told it. Or maybe it's just the truth about
me.

LIZ: Maybe it is the truth about you.

KOSTAS: [*nods*] A stiff dick with a human sewn on at the
balls. It depresses me.

LIZ: When I was nineteen one of my boyfriends killed himself.

KOSTAS: Because of you?

LIZ: He found out about one of my other lovers. I was upset,
but I wasn't shattered. I should have been shattered.

KOSTAS: Part of your scorecard. One suicide, five broken
marriages - - in your own mind it's no more than you're
worth.

LIZ: [*upset*] Don't Kostas!

KOSTAS: It's truth time.

LIZ: I'm not going to do it any more. I'm going to stop.

KOSTAS: You can't. You're hooked. Same as me.

LIZ: I want to stop.

KOSTAS: I want to stop too, but we won't. Not for years and years. Not until we feel the options starting to run out and hey, maybe we did want a family after all.

> [KOSTAS *looks at* LIZ. *There's a pause.*]

KOSTAS: There is another side to me. It's just not very developed.

LIZ: What?

KOSTAS: Kostas the Romantic.

LIZ: Not very developed at all.

KOSTAS: He started as a front for Kostas the Predator, but occasionally he takes over.

LIZ: What does he do?

KOSTAS: He gets this urge to save beautiful maidens.

LIZ: And then what?

KOSTAS: Return them to their castle and worship them from afar.

LIZ: And that's it?

KOSTAS: Maybe one of them pines for him and they have a courtship and they get married and he becomes Prince.

LIZ: And they live happily ever after?

KOSTAS: [*shakes head*] He gets bored, flies off to the Philippines forgets to use a condom and dies of Aids.

LIZ: Did you - -

KOSTAS: Use a condom? Every time. Some guys use two in case one breaks.

LIZ: Wouldn't be very sensitive would it?

KOSTAS: These aren't very sensitive guys.

LIZ: Is it just very mechanical? With these girls?

KOSTAS: I'm going to tell you something that you can choose to believe or not believe. Some of them had real orgasms.

LIZ: [*scoffing*] Kostas.

KOSTAS: I know it's not supposed to happen but the truth is some of them are bad little tarts who love sex. The world is a lot more awful than nice people want to believe.

LIZ: You're more awful than anyone could believe.

KOSTAS: How are you going to get out of this now? Paul's gone bananas over you and this other guy's here. [*Pause*] And the truth is you want to go to bed with me.

LIZ: That would really solve my problems wouldn't it.

KOSTAS: Actually it would. For a start I'm not married so you wouldn't be wrecking anyone else but me. [*Beat*] And I've been crazy about you since I first saw you.

LIZ: [*ironically*] I've noticed.

KOSTAS: You were giving all the signs to Paul. I took this as an enormous insult. I'm Greek. [*Pause*] You think I'm joking. I'm not. I'm crazy about you.

LIZ: What have we got here? Kostas the Romantic, or Kostas the Predator posing as Kostas the Romantic.

KOSTAS: Kostas the Truthful. First appearance.

[LIZ *and* KOSTAS *look at each other.*]

LIZ: Kostas, I'm really attracted to you and I think I have been for some time, but the most lunatic thing I could possibly do at this point in time would be to do anything about it.

[*to audience*] So of course I did. Not immediately. I went back to my room and lay awake for hours. I wondered why it was that when I had no one else to turn to, I went to him. Maybe because he was flawed like I was. And he was honest about it. I phoned him. He was waiting for the call.

[*The lights go down and go up in* LIZ's *room.* ROB *is lying on the bed reading. There's a knock on the door.* ROB *calls out 'Come in.'* PAUL *enters. He stares at* ROB.]

PAUL: What are you doing in Liz's room?

ROB: Because the room I share with Kostas is unavailable.

PAUL: Why?

ROB: I do not know why. I knocked on the door and Kostas told me to piss off. I told him I needed to sleep somewhere and he told me to sleep in Liz's room.

PAUL: Liz's room?

ROB: Yep. [*Pause*] Face it Paul. The woman is a nymphomaniac. And Kostas is into everything he can lay his hands on.

PAUL: [*to audience*] Angry, stunned. I can't remember what I was. Astounded? No probably more angry than anything else. At both of them.

ROB: [*to* PAUL] What are you going to do about Kostas? He's going to do the swap sometime tomorrow morning. Fifty thousand dollars cash.

PAUL: We'll get him.

[*The lights fade and go up in* KOSTAS's *room. Morning.* KOSTAS *is finishing dressing.* LIZ *has already dressed.*]

LIZ: I guess everybody is going to know.

KOSTAS: Why shouldn't they?

LIZ: I suppose in one way it's a relief.

KOSTAS: Stuff em.

LIZ: [*to audience*] The morning after Kostas and I slept together I tried to pretend the experience had been euphoric. I sincerely wanted it to be euphoric. Unfortunately our night of passion was a fiasco. A tentative, fumbling, embarrassing fiasco.

KOSTAS: [*to audience*] The morning after I felt really down. Kostas, king of the bedroom, practically impotent. She came at me like a jet at takeoff. The more I tried the worse it got. And this was the woman I'd wanted above all others?

LIZ: I'm going to talk to Paul and try and explain about us.

KOSTAS: [*sharply*] Explain what?

LIZ: You and me.

KOSTAS: Why does it need to be explained?

LIZ: Because contrary to what some people around here might think, I'm not in the habit of sleeping with two men at once.

KOSTAS: Are you going back to him?

LIZ: Of course not.

KOSTAS: What about you and me?

LIZ: That's up to you.

KOSTAS: I'm not normally like that.

LIZ: Like what?

KOSTAS: Like last night.

LIZ: Obviously it's me.

KOSTAS: The whole thing was probably a mistake.

LIZ: Maybe you should stick to prostitutes.

[KOSTAS *glares at her. There's a knock at the door.*
KOSTAS *goes to get it. He opens it partially then widens.*
ROB *walks in. He looks at the two of them.*]

KOSTAS: What's wrong with you?

ROB: [*coldly*] I thought you two were supposed to hate each
other?

KOSTAS: That's always the way Rob.

ROB: Paul got himself well and truly drunk last night. He's
not in great shape.

LIZ: I'm going to talk to him. [*She goes.*]

ROB: Give us the tape. I'll do the pick up.

KOSTAS: Forget it.

ROB: Forget it? Forget fifty thousand bucks? Are you kidding?

KOSTAS: Forget it.

[ROB *rummages in the drawer and grabs the tape.*]

ROB: Is this it?

KOSTAS: Give it to Paul.

ROB: Like hell I will! You set this thing up and I want my
money and you're going to take yours. Eleven o'clock at
the golf course fence, three miles out of town, right.

KOSTAS: [*indicating tape*] Give it to Paul.

ROB: Once you see the money you'll change your mind.

KOSTAS: No way. Give it to Paul!

ROB: You'll change your mind when you see the money.
[*to audience*] Kostas got a bit hesitant at the last moment,
but I knew he still wanted it, and I was determined to get
him. I'd been clean all my life and I wanted some
recognition of that. I wanted a headline and a photo of that
randy Greek being led off to jail where he belonged. And
we would get headlines. Much bigger than anything we'd
get for Billy Nottle.
[*He goes. The lights fade, and go up in* PAUL's *room.
He's sitting on the bed looking as if he's had a long hard
night on the bottle. There's a knock on the door and he
goes and gets it. He opens it and* LIZ *comes in. He nods
at her and goes back to sitting on the bed. She stays
standing.*]

LIZ: I'm sorry, but I'm glad it happened before anything got
out of hand with us.

PAUL: Were you just playing games or what?

LIZ: Not with you. I honestly didn't expect it to go that far. I feel terrible.

PAUL: It's not going to go away for me. I just can't turn off the tap.

LIZ: I'm really sorry. I'll resign as soon as we get back.

PAUL: Is this thing with Kostas serious?

LIZ: I don't know. It was probably just a futile attempt to break a pattern.

PAUL: What sort of pattern?

LIZ: A pattern of deceit. I've been doing it since I was fifteen. Game's over.

PAUL: It's wrecked me.

LIZ: I'm not feeling great either.

PAUL: You want Kostas, you have him.

LIZ: Paul.

PAUL: [*outburst*] Just get out, will you. Get out!

> [*Lights fade and go up again. Still* PAUL's *room. Midday.* ROB *bursts in.*]

ROB: Got it. Gave him a copy of the tape and got the full fifty thousand.

> [*He shows* PAUL *two bundles of hundred dollar notes.*]

PAUL: Got yourself wired up?

> [ROB *pats his lapel.*]

ROB: [*eagerly*] All set to go.

PAUL: Get the bastard.

ROB: [*grins*] With pleasure.

> [*Lights fade. Up again on* KOSTAS's *room.* ROB *enters. There's a sense of* ROB *maneuvering himself and the conversation in order to get the most incriminating recording.*]

Got it.

> [*He pulls the money out from under his coat.*]

Half for you. Half for me.

KOSTAS: [*angrily*] You crazy bastard.

ROB: Hey, this was your idea.

KOSTAS: I told you not to do it.

ROB: Twenty five thousand each. No sweat.

> [ROB *throws him his half.* KOSTAS, *in reflex, catches it.*]

KOSTAS: I told you not to do it. I told you to give the tape to Paul.

ROB: Amazing feeling isn't it. Twenty five grand in your hand?

[KOSTAS *looks at the money, feels it.*]

KOSTAS: It's not exactly going to solve the country's problems if Nottle goes to jail, is it?

ROB: Too late to send him to jail now. He's got the tape. You can burn your money if you like, but we can't give it back.

KOSTAS: Jesus, what I could do with this.

ROB: It's yours. You set up the deal. Take your cut.

[KOSTAS *hesitates.*]

KOSTAS: You sure we're going to get away with this?

ROB: Who in the hell is ever going to know?

[KOSTAS *pockets the money and heads for the door.* ROB *positions himself in such a way as to get a clear recording.*]

Be careful. Don't suddenly put the whole twenty-five thousand into your bank account.

KOSTAS: I'm not an idiot.

[*He exits. The lights fade and come up in* PAUL's *room.* PAUL *is sitting there waiting. There's a knock. He leaps to his feet and is surprised to see* KOSTAS *enter.* KOSTAS *is highly emotional.*]

Two things. Yeah, I fucked Liz. The reason? I'm crazy about her. Have been since I saw her. It didn't work out, it's probably been a giant foul up, but there you go. I'm not sorry and I'm not going to apologise. If you want to hit me hit me.

[PAUL *stares at him.*]

Second thing. I lied to you. I got Nottle to talk and he offered me a bribe.

[*He throws the twenty five thousand dollars on* PAUL's *bed.*]

Now that lunatic Rob has gone and sold the tape, and he's trying to get me to take half the proceeds.

[ROB *comes in the room. He sees the money on the bed. He looks at* PAUL. PAUL *looks at* KOSTAS.]

ROB: You're gone Kostas old son.

KOSTAS: What the fuck are you talking about?

ROB: I'm talking about five to ten years you slime.

> [*He takes a tape recorder from his coat.*]

We've got you loud and clear accepting a twenty five thousand dollar bribe.

KOSTAS: I just came here to tell Paul, you dickhead.

ROB: Too late, shitfeatures. We've got the whole thing on tape.

KOSTAS: You pushed this right from the start!

ROB: No way. It was your idea, I just picked up the cash. It's all right here.

> [KOSTAS *turns to* PAUL.]

KOSTAS: I just came to tell you about it!

PAUL: [*with venomous satisfaction*] Did you? I didn't hear a thing.

KOSTAS: [*angry*] Hey, listen! This is not on! This is a frame!

PAUL: You'll be formally charged when we get back to the city. Don't try and skip off anywhere.

KOSTAS: [*to audience*] Well at that stage, I was feeling as if I was pretty much stuffed. My career steps were going to be fairly limited after five years or more inside. I went to see Liz and things got worse.

> [*Lights fade and up again in* LIZ's *room.* SHARON, *the receptionist is waiting there with a shotgun. He knocks and* SHARON *moves across and opens the door.*]

Sharon?

SHARON: Get over there!

KOSTAS: Sharon, I'm in enough shit already without getting shot!

SHARON: I started thinking about suicide, and then I started thinking, no. I'm not going to kill myself, I'm going to kill the bastard who caused it.

KOSTAS: Sharon, you'll go to prison for the rest of your life. I'm not worth it.

SHARON: Stand up against the wall.

KOSTAS: If you're going to shoot me, shoot me here.

SHARON: Stand up against the wall!

> [KOSTAS *moves against the wall.*]

KOSTAS: Sharon I'll marry you. I promise. I'm not married to
Liz. That was just for this thing we were doing. I'm free.
I'm available. I'm a bachelor. I got an M.B.A. [*Pause*] I
will have my M.B.A. In a year. Sharon I mean it. I'll marry
you!

SHARON: I wouldn't marry you if your farts smelled like
violets !
[*She aims at his head and slowly begins to pull the
trigger.*]

KOSTAS: [*panic stricken*] Sharon, for Christ's sake! You'll go
to prison for life!

SHARON: I'm not going to get caught. I got Greg outside
waiting for the gun and by the time they find your body
I'll be back behind the desk.

KOSTAS: You'll have to answer to God!

SHARON: I'm an atheist.

KOSTAS: Sharon! For Christ's sake don't shoot!

SHARON: I'll shoot all right. I just want to see you suffer a
bit first.
[SHARON *sniffs the air.*]

SHARON: Ever shat your pants before, lover boy?

KOSTAS: Sharon, for Christ's sake.
[SHARON *aims and slowly pulls the trigger. The gun
clicks, but there's no explosion.*]

SHARON: It isn't loaded.

KOSTAS: [*sinking to the ground with relief*] Jesus Sharon.

SHARON: I'm marrying Greg.

KOSTAS: That's great. That's really great.

SHARON: And if he ever sees you again up here he'll punch
your head in.

KOSTAS: I don't think I'll be here again for quite a while.
[LIZ *comes in the door and sees* SHARON *brandishing the
shotgun at* KOSTAS.]

LIZ: Sharon!

KOSTAS: It's not loaded.

SHARON: [*to* LIZ] If it was there'd be one in here for you too.
[*She walks out, slamming the door.*]

LIZ: Migod.

KOSTAS: Sharon's the least of my worries.

LIZ: What's happened?

KOSTAS: I'll tell you when I've had a shower.

　　　[KOSTAS *retreats shamefaced towards the bathroom.*]

LIZ: [*to audience*] What I really would be good at is espionage. All you need is to trust in the fact that when something stirs below the belt, the male I.Q. drops fifty points.

　　　[*The lights fade and come up in* ROB's *room. Evening. He's in his dressing gown whistling happily. There is a knock on the door. He opens it.* LIZ *comes in.*]

　Hi.

ROB: Hi.

LIZ: Have you seen Paul?

ROB: No.

LIZ: Is Kostas in some kind of trouble? He won't talk to me.

ROB: Kostas took a bribe from Billy Nottle. Kostas is going to jail.

LIZ: Took a bribe?

ROB: Your boyfriend took a bribe. We got it on tape.

LIZ: [*shakes her head*] He's not my boyfriend.

ROB: You just go to bed with anyone?

LIZ: Don't Rob. I made a stupid mistake. Don't make me feel worse.

ROB: You admit it.

LIZ: I feel so ashamed.

ROB: Why Kostas?

LIZ: God knows. The men I'm attracted to I never sleep with and the ones I'm not attracted to I do.

ROB: Why?

LIZ: My therapist says it's fear of commitment. If there's someone I'm really attracted to I might fall in love and then I wouldn't have power over them any more. Make sense?

ROB: That's why I got the flick?

LIZ: Let's leave that.

ROB: I know when women are attracted to me and when they aren't, and you were attracted.

LIZ: Rob, I don't want to talk about it.

ROB: I think we should.

LIZ: [*nods*] All right. It's true.
 [ROB *nods his head.*]
ROB: You've been hot for me for a long time.
LIZ: It's true.
ROB: I got you nine tenths there and you backed off.
LIZ: [*nods*] It's a pattern.
ROB: It's a pattern you're going to have to break.
LIZ: Yeah.
ROB: Soon.
LIZ: Yeah.
ROB: Really soon. What d'you want to drink?
 [*He moves to her and stares into her eyes. She stares back, then moves across and sits down.*]
LIZ: Gin and tonic. Kostas took a bribe? And you've got it on tape?
ROB: Yeah, have a listen.
 [*He moves across and takes a tape out of his drawer, slips it into a microcassette player, and begins to play it. The lights fade and come up in* LIZ's *room. Evening.* KOSTAS *sits, agitated on the bed. There's a knock on the door. He opens it and* PAUL *comes in. The two men stare at each other.*]
PAUL: I'm going to drop the charges. You came to me with the money before Rob arrived.
 [KOSTAS *slumps on the bed in relief.*]
KOSTAS: I mentioned the offer and he encouraged me to go for it. When I said no he just kept charging on.
PAUL: I actually took money for a year when I was in the vice squad. I know how it can happen.
KOSTAS: You've got to believe me. Rob was urging me on.
PAUL: [*nods*] He wanted to get you.
KOSTAS: [*suddenly, urgently*] Talking of Rob.
 [*He phones urgently. No answer.*]
 Shit! Phone's off the hook.
PAUL: Who are you ringing? Rob?
KOSTAS: Liz is down there trying to get the tape.
PAUL: From Rob?
KOSTAS: Yeah, Mata Hari. I couldn't stop her.
PAUL: [*disdainfully*] Rob?

KOSTAS: Yeah, makes me sick too.
    [Gets up and moves towards the door.]
  I'll go down and bash his fucking door down.
PAUL: Let her get it.
KOSTAS: You kidding? You're going to drop the charges.
PAUL: If he's got it he can still make trouble. That's the thing
  I'm really worried about. It's there on tape that you took
  a bribe and there's only my word for what happened
  afterwards. He's so vindictive he could try and destroy both
  of us.
KOSTAS: I can't leave her down there with that slime!
PAUL: She won't screw him. She can't stand the guy.
KOSTAS: *[not quite convinced]* Yeah, that's true.
PAUL: Let her try and get it. She'll think of something.
    *[Lights down. They go up again. We're still in LIZ's room
    but PAUL is gone. It's early morning. KOSTAS is alone,
    pacing agitatedly around the room. The door opens and
    LIZ comes in. LIZ looks at KOSTAS, pulls a microtape out
    of her pocket and throws it to KOSTAS.]*
KOSTAS: Did you have to - -?
LIZ: Only way I could get him to sleep. Sorry, I'll take a
  shower.
KOSTAS: *[holding up the tape]* Thanks.
LIZ: *[to audience]* The awful thing, the thing I've never told
  anybody, is that I got more excited with that sleazebag than
  I had for years. I'm sure it was just the excitement of
  deception. As soon as it was over I loathed him more than
  ever, and couldn't bear the thought of going near him again.
KOSTAS: *[to audience]* The thing that really hurt was that the
  bastard asked me for his hundred dollars the next morning.
  The thing I really enjoyed was hitting him.
    *[LIZ exits for the shower. There's a knock on the door.
    KOSTAS goes to get it. STEVEN, LIZ's married lover comes
    in.]*
STEVEN: Who are you?
KOSTAS: I don't think you really want to know.
STEVEN: Where's Liz?
KOSTAS: In the shower. And when she comes out she's going
  to bed with me.

STEVEN: Who are you?

KOSTAS: I'm her brother. It's the thing she didn't want you to know.

STEVEN: She hasn't got a brother.

KOSTAS: Is your family wrecked beyond repair?

STEVEN: Beyond repair? Are you joking? Last I heard my wife was shopping round for a hit man.

KOSTAS: Go home bearing gifts. Prostrate yourself. Crawl. Kiss her feet. Do anything, no matter how demeaning or how painful. In a matter of only years you may be forgiven.

STEVEN: She won't have me back.

KOSTAS: Try, Steven. You've got no hope here.

STEVEN: I want to hear that from her.

[KOSTAS *nods, goes into the bathroom, calls* LIZ. *She comes out in her bathrobe.*]

KOSTAS: I've told Steven to go back to his wife. He wants to hear it from you.

LIZ: Go back to your wife Steven. I've fallen in love with Kostas and we're going to be married.

STEVEN: That's it?

LIZ: That's absolutely and utterly it.

[*to audience*]

That wasn't quite it of course. Kostas and I are still not married, but we are living together which is a huge breakthrough for me.

KOSTAS: [*to audience*] We get on each other's nerves and fight and she threatens to leave and I threaten to leave, but we're still together.

LIZ: [*to audience*] There's something deep inside which still draws me to guys with power and money, but I haven't succumbed.

KOSTAS: [*to audience*] She hasn't succumbed because I'd smash her. And when I'm out of town there's still a tendency for me to pick up the phone book and flick through the pages to 'Escort Agencies' but I've never succumbed.

LIZ: [*to audience*] Because I'd smash him. I'm back part time finishing a degree in - Oh God it's so boring - commerce and accounting, but at least I'll be able to do something.

KOSTAS: [*to audience*] She's getting first class honours. Better than I ever did.

LIZ: [*to audience*] I'm going to be a film producer, or an investment adviser. I don't want to get tacky, but I think you should know that our sex life is getting to be really something.

KOSTAS: [*to audience*] Getting to be? Thanks. I'm working in a law firm because the Task Force against Corruption was dismantled. I deal mainly with divorce.

PAUL: [*to audience*] I'm back in the police force. The Task Force Against Corruption was dismantled by the government when we started on the trail of some very unorthodox tendering in their own public works department. I had some strong words to say to the media when it happened. There's no way I'm going to get to be chief commissioner.

SHARON: [*to audience*] I married Greg and the bastard got me pregnant and pissed off. Now he wants to come back and I'm not going to have him.

ROB: [*to audience*] I resigned from the Task Force months before it was disbanded and made it clear to the press why. Paul's investigation of government tendering was spurious and motivated by malice and I said so. I'm back in the police force and in the running to be chief commissioner.

STEVEN: [*to audience*] My wife refused to have me back. The bitch. I'm having an affair with a chiropractor who's an expert in Italian frescoes. I'm taking her to Tuscany.

BILLY NOTTLE: [*to audience*] I was found guilty of conspiracy and guilty of attempted bribery. But it was only a white collar crime so I only got six months. I retired to Sanctuary Cove.

LIZ: [*to audience*] So there you have it. I'm not quite sure what you'll make of all this. To my way of thinking it's a contemporary love story of sorts.

[*Lights fade on the cast.*]

END OF PLAY.